THE HORSEMAN'S GUIDE TO THE MEANING OF LIFE

Lessons I've Learned From Horses, Horsemen, and Other Heroes

DON BURT

FOREWORD BY STEVEN D. PRICE

Skyhorse Publishing

Skyhorse Publishing books may be purchased in bulk at special discounts for sales promotion, corporate gifts, fund-raising, or educational purposes. Special editions can also be created to specifications. For details, contact the Special Sales Department, Skyhorse Publishing, 307 West 36th Street, 11th Floor, New York, NY 10018 or info@skyhorsepublishing.com.

Skyhorse® and Skyhorse Publishing® are registered trademarks of Skyhorse Publishing, Inc.®, a Delaware corporation.

Visit our website at www.skyhorsepublishing.com.

10 9 8 7 6 5 4 3 2 1

Library of Congress Cataloging-in-Publication Data

Burt, Don.
 The horseman's guide to the meaning of life : lessons I've learned from horses, horsemen, and other heroes / Don Burt.
    p. cm.
 ISBN 978-1-60239-661-6
 1. Burt, Don. 2. Horse trainers--United States--Biography.
 3. Horsemanship. 4. Self-evaluation. 5. Life skills. I. Title.
 SF284.52.B87A3 2009
 636.1092--dc22
 [B]

                                    2009006051

Cover design by Tom Lau
Cover image credit: iStock.com/Yuri_Arcurs

Print ISBN: 978-1-5107-3154-7
Ebook ISBN: 978-1-5107-3156-1

Printed in China

Contents

Foreword by Steven D. Price

When Tony Lyons asked me to find someone to write the equestrian volume for Skyhorse's "Guide to the Meaning of Life" series, I didn't have to think very long or hard to come up with Don Burt as the ideal candidate. In all my years of reading, riding, writing, and editing, I hadn't encountered anyone in the horse world who came close to Don's knowledge and appreciation of that world and from so many perspectives (at one point he was licensed to judge every breed and discipline recognized by the American Horse Shows Association). And, since this was to be a book, Don was equally adept at setting down entertaining and instructive yarns about his experiences.

I met Don in the late 1980s when his agent submitted a proposal to the publisher for whom I worked at the time. *Winning with Arabian Horses* seemed like an eminently viable idea, and we jumped at it. When I phoned Don to introduce myself after we signed up the project, he was kind enough to invite me to visit him and his wife, Ardys, for a few days at their Southern California home. Don lived up to his agent's advanced billing: a professional and personal pleasure to work with and, to my great pleasure, a wonderful riding companion. One morning's hack took us to a bluff overlooking Catalina Island in the distance and in the foreground two whales sounding in the Pacific Ocean channel (in my experience, a very rare sight from horseback).

Several years later, Don phoned with another invitation: how would I like to do public relations for an Arabian horse farm in Kentucky that's owned by a Japanese businessman? Unable to decline such a piquant request, I agreed, and for a few days every month for almost two years I joined Don and several other farm advisors at the facility outside Louisville. That gave me ample opportunity to observe Don's eye for horses and his horsemanship abilities. "Everything I learned about horses, I learned from horses," Don told us more than once. "Teach yourself not to look but to see, and not just to hear but to listen."

Don also regaled us with tales from his youth, such as when a cowhand showed up at his father's stable. "I hear a feller who can ride some can make a living in the movies hereabouts," the stranger said. In exchange for doing barn chores, the cowhand stayed at the stable until he broke into the movies, first as John Wayne's stunt double and then as the Oscar-winning actor Ben Johnson. Or when the actor Robert Taylor, whom Don taught to ride for the Walt Disney film *Miracle of the White Stallions*, helped Don convince prospective customers to buy horses.

Don's administrative and interpersonal skills came into play when he served on the American Quarter Horse Association's executive board and became its president in 1996 (his book *Winning with the American Quarter Horse* remains an essential guide to showing and judging the breed). At Don's urging I wrote two books for AQHA, during the course of which I spent time at the association's headquarters in Amarillo, Texas. Everyone to whom I spoke there had nothing but good things to say about Don's leadership and motivational skills as well as his curiosity and enthusiasm for all aspects of equestrian competition and recreation.

Don also advised the American Horse Shows Association and the United States Equestrian Team, both of whose former executive Chrystine Tauber called him "an extraordinary horseman whose extensive knowledge and leadership influenced our entire sport. He was a great mediator and consensus builder. When I was at the AHSA and the Team, Don was our 'go to' man for negotiations. His efforts, including introducing reining to the USET Festival of Champions, allowed our visions to become reality. For many decades, Don was my trusted advisor and cherished friend."

Don's death six years ago deprived his many friends and fans of sharing more of his good humor, good sense, and sound philosophy. We are, however, grateful for this book, a distillation of his life and lore and a celebration of the animals and the people he admired and learned so much from—English and Western riders, trainers, officials, and horse-lovers from all over the country and indeed the world. By the same token, readers involved in the horse world in any capacity will learn much from *The Horseman's Guide to the Meaning of Life*—not only about their animals, but also about themselves.

Steven D. Price
New York, NY
March 2018

Acknowledgments

In my life, there have been many people who have influenced me and several who have played an integral part in the successes I may have achieved. Some were actual mentors. This book is a compilation of teachings or lessons I learned from them. Their names are too numerous to list individually.

Besides my faithful friend and literary advisor, Steven D. Price, there are two other people who deserve recognition, one being my dad. His deeds and the way he lived his life was his gift to me. Resilience is a word he really never used but lived each day. It gave him the power to overcome adversity. He did have a saying that was not always easy to achieve—*Let no one outwork you today*—which says a lot about those who have found success.

The other person to whom I owe much of the success I have enjoyed and who, by thought, word, and deed, has been my guiding light and is always there for me and who took her wedding vows to heart is my wife, Ardys. Her name should appear on the cover with mine, because we truly are a team.

Introduction

I have tried to organize my wandering thoughts into the many events, horses, and people that have helped mold my life, both successes and failures. From earning my first merit badge (horsemanship) and becoming an Eagle Scout to the hills I've climbed and the stages I've stood on to receive awards and recognition, it's been a great ride.

Every arena in the world has a story. No matter what they are called, nor their size or shape, they play a major part in all of our lives. They are where battles are fought and history is made. From race tracks and sports arenas to Olympic venues, whoever wins or loses becomes both public and private. They are memories in our own personal file that we can relive throughout our lives.

Horses, too, have played a significant role in my life and, if you look back in history, in the lives of most everyone. Horses are a lot like people: some you relate to immediately and some you are wary of. Being able to communicate is the key to their understanding. Some enjoy pressure, others are afraid of it, and in life we learn to adjust as they do. All horses and people teach you something if you take the time to listen and learn. Both issue challenges at every turn.

Family is another necessary part of success. Family to me doesn't have to mean blood relation; it can include others in the same endeavor, business, or pursuit. Families are there to pick you up when you're down or take you down a peg when you're flying too high. Success is often fleeting; family and memories last forever. As I have grown older and no longer can compete physically, my mind still remains pretty much on course. This is the time to relive, to dream once again (never give up on your dreams) of what was, what is, and what might be.

As I assembled my memories and put them on paper, I relived each one and reflected often on the phrases and quotes that ring so true. There are an abundance of happy times and even a few tears, but I wouldn't change any of it. The lessons I've learned that I pass on and the people I've met along the way are the true meaning of life to me. I am forever grateful.

The Way
I Remember It

Since I could walk, the longest time I've ever been without a horse of some kind was about three days. This occurred when I had to sell my horse in order to buy my first car. Not wasting any time, I went to the next auction, did some wheeling and dealing, and came home with a horse, which I traded a couple of days later for one that I really wanted. Even when I was serving my time in the U.S. Navy, I always had a good horse somewhere to ride.

When I was little, I didn't know anyone who didn't have a horse. A native Californian raised in Burbank, California, the horse capital of the western United States, I thought everyone had horses. Burbank was the hub of the horse business; every lot was occupied by one house and a two- or three-stall barn or corral. One section known as the "river bottom," along Riverside

Drive, was the home to great horsemen. On one end of the mile-long row of stables was the Hitching Post Saloon, once owned by actor Hoot Gibson, a home away from home to actors and stuntmen. On the opposite end was the Amble Inn, owned by rodeo greats Jerry Ambler and Wag Blessing. This area was my playground, and virtually every great horseman of that era, whether Hollywood actor or professional, put in some time there.

Even today, amidst the sprawling metropolis of Los Angeles, Burbank has remained virtually intact. The Los Angeles Equestrian Center occupies most of the old stable locations, including my father's and grandfather's. The center has become a drawing card for the many Hollywood personalities who embrace the show world of horses, and Riverside Drive is still a place where you buy a house because of the stable in the backyard. I remember riding across the swinging bridge spanning the Los Angeles River into the vast trail system of Griffith Park when I was about five; it is still used daily for trail rides. Though not as busy as it once was, the Pickwick Coffee Shop remains open, offering the echoes of trainers, shoers, movie extras, and rodeo greats. A few lease and boarding stables and tack shops remain next to the center, along with condos that are also equipped to take care of your horse.

My father and grandfather were both horse trainers, and I had envisioned myself carrying on in their footsteps. Of course, my mother had other ambitions for my career, but I was also a little headstrong. She once told me, "Son, you'll either be president or a janitor … I only hope it isn't the latter." I, of course, knew she was comparing horse training to a janitor type of existence, but I paid little heed to her words and persevered in my love of horses. With an angel on each shoulder, I seem to have moved through life and its plateaus with a new adventure at every turn. Even when faced with adversity, another door would miraculously spring open for me, even though at the time I thought my life was over.

Having grown up in the arena, surrounded by shows and chaos, it took many years to start to appreciate a more relaxed life that wasn't governed by a time schedule. My twilight years have allowed me the freedom to take the time to trace the steps of the Indians and study how they lived and traveled. I've discovered a great interest in the large ranches that use horses in their daily operations; they made this country what it is. Having grown up where movie sets were the norm, I'm learning the real stories behind covered wagons, chuck wagons, and roping your horse from the remuda— true-to-life cowboying up. What I always thought were ponds (no matter the size) have instead become troughs, tanks, or lakes (in Texas, that is). I've formed a new appreciation for forgotten sayings like "As long as the grass grows and the wind blows." As I look back, I've seen many changes take place in the horse industry throughout my career. I've survived over three-quarters of a century and played cowboy all my life. I don't feel like I've ever worked a day.

The Arena Was My Home

Throughout my life and career, the arena has been the marketplace, where you show your wares and demonstrate your talents and abilities. When I was young, the arena might have consisted of only an empty lot with a rope for boundaries. As the years went by, the arena became more sophisticated; today many are like stadiums. But it is still the marketplace. We had match races, bush tracks, and modern racetracks, but the arena was more personal to the spectators, and it has always been the source of business and its rewards.

During my life, I think I spent more time in an arena than anywhere else. It can be used literally or abstractly and has always been a place to judge or be judged. My personality came to the fore one time when I was showing in a jumping class at the Cow Palace. It was a five-foot-high class, which consisted of four single-rail fences that you jumped over twice. In those days rubs against the rails counted, along with knock-downs and refusals: one fault for a front touch and one half fault for a hind rub. I was clean up to the last fence. As my horse left the ground, he jumped off to the left by the arena wall, where a lady was hanging over the rail to get a good look. At the peak of the fence, she and I were nose to nose, so close I could have kissed her. She screamed and fell back into her box seat as my horse gave an extra thrust to clear the obstacle. I was hanging off the horse's side but made it through the finish line before I fell off. It was the only clean round, and I bowed to the deafening applause, blew the lady a kiss, and remounted to accept the trophy.

When judging, it was important to stand in a corner where I could see most of the arena. This all became apparent with experience. Whether a class was held in a large, small, or peculiarly shaped arena, indoors or outside, played a part in how easy I could make the class, or how difficult. Even now when I'm outside of the arena I analyze my surroundings: a room, a building, the ocean, or a rushing stream—reading them all is just like reading the arena. We are aware of our surroundings every day, driving on the freeway or riding in a crowded elevator—not only of the physical layout or structure but of those sharing the space. Most accidents occur when you're not paying attention.

When judging, you must expect the unexpected and not rush to a judicial decision. I was judging a championship show in São Paulo, Brazil (my first trip to South America). The show was held in a large stadium used for soccer, track and field, and several other sports. This particular class was a pleasure-driving class with ten horses—nine Brazilian competitors and one American horse that had been brought in just for the occasion. The class was held on a half-mile oval track encompassing the arena, made up of some mixture of cinder and dirt material.

I had the class trot, extend the trot, walk—all the required gaits. As I was busily keeping my notes and sorting out the class, my ringmaster, also my chaperone and translator, kept hovering over my shoulder. Suddenly he said, "Oh, no, no!" Usually I never say a word to the ringmaster; in fact I never let them get that close. "What?" I questioned. On my list from the first direction around the arena, I had the American horse on top, followed by the nine Brazilians. The ringmaster told me the last judge from America had placed an American first and the crowd went wild, jumping the fence and beating up on the judge. "He's by far the best horse," I replied, and I then told him to reverse the class to travel clock-wise. With the ringmaster trying to save my life and me trying not to be intimidated by the thought of being beaten up by a mob, I kept my cool.

It was getting late afternoon, and shadows were forming right in front of the standing-room-only grand-stand full of Brazilian spectators. As the horses were making their passes, a light standard cast a shadow across the track. As the American horse approached, he spooked, leapt over the shadow, broke his gait, and ran off, jerking the buggy to pieces. I simply crossed out his number and silently said, "Thank you, Lord. I'll take it from here."

Sometimes while judging, things don't turn out as you had hoped. One such faux pas happened a couple of years before the 1984 Olympic Games were to be held in Los Angeles. The Japanese, fielding a team for the first time, sent their team to the United States to become acclimated, buy horses, and learn as much as possible before the games.

They arrived in the spring and had a schedule of horse shows on their agenda. One show was part of a cir-cuit in Michigan, held only a week or so after they had arrived. During that week, they bought several horses: some good, some not so good. Being newcomers, they attracted some questionable horse dealers, who were ready to sell them a horse. They picked up some mounts that were great to look at but quite professional in being able to unseat a rider at the last moment.

It came time for the grand prix competition, which is usually held the last afternoon of the show. Three of us were to comprise the jury: two to watch for faults and one to handle the timer. As luck would have it, I was chosen president of the jury; one of my duties was to accept the salute from the riders and salute them in return, which is a signal to begin.

The course was designed by an English woman named Pamela Carruthers, a master in the fine art of designing courses for horse shows, grand prix, and international show-jumping competitions. The riders walked the course with their respective *chefs d'equipe* (coaches), discussing strategy, direction, strides, and so on. Thirty horses were entered; the weather was perfect, and the crowd looked on enthusiastically. Pamela had figured about ten clear rounds to ensure a good jump-off, and she usually guaranteed the spectators an entertaining class.

The first of the Japanese riders to go was turned out in white britches, a scarlet coat with a blue collar, and highly polished boots. His horse was equally presentable. When the rider's name was announced, no one was aware that he was royalty—a real prince. The horse he rode looked familiar, but I couldn't quite jog my memory. I stood up and bowed in return to his hat-off salute.

The horn sounded, and the prince headed for the first fence, a 4'9" brush-and-rail oxer. All went well. The next two fences, a gate and a double-square oxer, were clean also. A solid brick wall with white poles on top reached a height of 5'4" and loomed in the distance. The rider charged down to the wall and kept on going, over the horse's head and into the wall. His mount had put her head down suddenly and catapulted the rider upside down. "Oh!" came the groan from the crowd and officials in unison. I then remembered the horse having dumped a few other riders in her time.

In some jumping classes, fall of horse and/or rider constitutes elimination. However, this particular class was governed by the Fédération Equestre Internationale (FEI). Under their rules, the rider may remount and continue and is penalized only on jumping faults and time.

The prince, slightly soiled but still presentable, gathered himself and walked to his horse, which stood patiently waiting. He faced the jury and bowed. I, being president, bowed in return. Hesitating a moment, he remounted and walked a few feet, turned, and raced toward the jump. The brakes screeched again, sending the prince hurling through the air and crashing into the wall. The horse stood quietly by, peering down at him. "Ouch!" I said out loud. "I'm sure he's had enough."

The prince struggled to his feet, brushed himself off, turned to the jury stand, and bowed. I returned another courtesy bow. He remounted and again repeated the routine—halt, somersault, and crash. He has to quit now, I thought. Three refusals and you're eliminated. He slowly got to his feet and painfully made his courteous bow from the waist. I reciprocated. But instead of exiting, he mounted and made a beeline for the wall that resulted in a total disaster; the prince was upside down and bleeding from the battering. Tottering, he rose once more and started to bow but a voice yelled out from behind us. "Wait! Wait! Don't bow, wait!" I turned to see an overexcited Japanese man in a turtleneck sweater, schooling boots, and britches elbowing his way to the stage. "Wait," he gasped. "Why do you try to kill prince?" We all looked at each other, dumbfounded. I realized he was the team's chef d'equipe, and everything stopped momentarily while we got to the bottom of the situation. It seems the competition rules that the Japanese are accustomed to say that when a rider wishes to withdraw, he simply faces the judges and bows. We, however, thought he wanted to continue on course or take a schooling fence after his three refusals. So I had returned a courtesy bow to indicate he should proceed (after all, he was royalty).

The poor prince, however, was only asking permission to be excused, to withdraw, go home, leave. By standing and bowing, I was telling him to remain on course. Being the gentleman he was, he continued to obey our command, which almost killed him and ignited World War III. The Japanese team is now one of the world's premier competitors. I, meanwhile, have wisely learned a few of their customs and even a bit of the language.

THE HORSEMAN'S CLASSROOM

I liken the arena to a classroom. You can never anticipate or even imagine what might take place. As I grew older and more experienced, I was able to read the arena: whether the footing (ground) was too hard, too soft, or (hopefully) just right, and to be aware of what was underfoot—cement, sand, rocks, or mud. I learned quickly to analyze the firmness of a foundation for just about any situation a horse could encounter. Then the variables were added: puddles, light and shadows, unevenness, and the changes to the arena after each use. Knowing how to use the arena and its variables to my best advantage became a plus—where to place the jumps and where to ask the horse to slide to a stop, turning cattle on the fence, or how far off the rail to stay. These insights helped in my life's decision making.

Getting There: Motivation and Inspiration

Some people dream of becoming doctors, lawyers, firemen, or G-men. My heroes have always been cowboys. From my first recollection, the horse has been my inspiration. I'd sit for hours just watching them and wondering why they did what they did. Of course, growing up in a family where horses were an integral part of everyday life probably contributed to my interest. (Although my brother, who grew up in the same environment, never wanted to look at another horse and hasn't to this day.) I was forever trying new things or seeing how much I could teach one to do. It was never work for me. Each day became a new challenge, and I couldn't wait to get to the barn, especially if a new horse had arrived.

When I was very young, I never really appreciated nor fully understood the saying, "When life gives you lemons, make lemonade," until I got a lemon. At the peak of my riding and training career, I was literally riding high. But a split-second decision changed all that. Late one afternoon, I stopped by my indoor arena to tell two little girls who were still riding their pony to be sure to turn out the lights before they left. Running into the arena, I found them trying to jump the pony (a big no-no when I wasn't there), and the pony was stopping at the fence. I yelled at them to stop and get off because they were going to get hurt and the pony was learning bad habits.

I couldn't let that happen, so I climbed aboard. Being in a hurry, I neglected to adjust the stirrups and proceeded toward the fence, the kind with a space in the top to insert brush. The pony stopped. I slapped his behind from my jockey-style position and tried it again. The pony started to stop but changed his mind and jumped straight up and down. In doing so, he stuck a foot between the slats and turned himself over on top of me. I listened to every crack as all the bones on my left side broke. As a result, my riding career was over, and my income quickly diminished.

In a cast for a lengthy duration, I spent my recovery putting to work my observations of the past.

A few years earlier, I had rescued a funny-colored two-year-old colt, mostly white and roan, that had been neglected. The owners just wanted to get rid of him. He had a white face with two huge dark eyes that reminded me of inkwells, and he was in poor shape physically. I took him home, cleaned him up, and put him in a training program for the next year. During this time, he was allowed to roam around, and once he even found his way into the house kitchen. He chased the chickens and broke down fences. He could open any stall door without a combination lock on it.

Then it was time for him to start earning his keep. As his breeding was doubtful, I schooled him for the open shows (any breed allowed), and he met this challenge with some success, showing first in hackamore classes and then as a Western pleasure horse in a bit. After the initial shock of the accident wore off, I found my interest in this horse increased. I spent long days trying to find out how much a horse could learn. I drew dots on him where I thought his reactors were. When I touched one dot, a foot would move; another spot, the head would turn or the tail would swish. I observed what made the horse respond and how. Having mastered the basic tricks—shake hands, count, say yes and no—the challenge level increased. Kneel, wave, and lay down were followed by antics not normally taught to a horse: roll over, crawl, sit down, play ball, and tag. It seemed there was no end to what this horse could learn and then do on command, with no halter, rope, or whip—strictly at liberty.

Though my peers had helped with judging jobs during the interim, after the casts were removed it was hard to start a new training stable while barely able to get around. One night, a car dealer on television was hammering away with his pitch, decked out in black cowboy clothes, wearing a black mask. He obviously needed something more, and my brain turned on the lightbulb. The next morning, I headed for the advertising agency that handled the account for Black Bart Motors and sold them on the idea of a sidekick for their masked client. Of course I had in mind my ol' white and roan horse with the inkwell eyes as his partner, and I spent the next day polishing all his tricks. A mask was made for the horse, as well as clothes like the car dealer's. What about a name? After much discussion, it was decided they would be Black Bart and Frosty. The camera rolled, on came the red light, and I held my breath. Frosty was great, and the commercial turned out to be better than the programs. After several weeks of live TV commercials with Frosty stealing the show, they were selling more cars than ever.

He was turned loose, and when the lights came on, he would ham it up for the cameras.

During the couple of years that followed, Frosty appeared at supermarket openings, entertained at schools and civic functions, led parades, and ended up with his own TV show on a local station: *Frosty's Farm Club*. His mask gave him powers, so the kids were told. On the show, he read the funnies, played "Frosty says," answered questions, did arithmetic problems, drank soda pop (pretending it was milk), and made a fool out of me as often as possible. The kids loved it. It went on to become the highest-rated children's show at that time.

I could have Frosty do almost anything because I had observed his reactions at the learning point, which extends to my philosophy today. Do your homework so you can analyze each situation with knowledge and make it fun.

His popularity grew. He did a stint in a well-known nightclub. He walked in all alone, went up to the bar for a drink, paid with special money, made his way through the crowd to the stage, did the hoochy-koochy dance with the showgirls, and left the way he came in. This act lasted for several months, along with several guest appearances at other clubs in the area.

One day, though, while being made up for a TV spot (they actually had to put bluing on Frosty's face so it would show up white on live TV), a wall collapsed behind Frosty and he had to be led outside. While waiting, he was longing for a little exercise, and that's when it happened. He stepped on something lodged in the ground and broke a bone in his foot that didn't heal for years. After a farewell party given by all those who loved him, he was turned out to pasture for a life of rest and green grass. Ironically, just before his accident Frosty had been considered for the role of Mister Ed in the TV series, a part he could have played to the hilt.

I've always thought determination should have been my middle name. My mother called it bullheadedness. But from the time I can remember, I would set goals for things I wanted to do, and nobody or nothing could talk me out of them. I know I learned it at an early age because my mother, an invalid most of my childhood, was actually an inspiration. She resolved to conquer both polio and meningitis, the combination of which left her unable to walk and blind for a while. Wanting to be self-reliant, she had my dad build three steps to nowhere. As her sight started to improve, she would spend hours in the backyard attempting to climb those stairs, hobbling on two canes. After falling down and refusing help, she'd attack the steps again and again. Once she mastered the first step, she moved on to the second and then the third. Bruised from constantly falling, she was determined to climb all three and come back down again without falling. This conquest made, she went through the same long ritual with one cane and then no cane at all. I can remember my dad each night massaging her legs and doctoring her bruises. But in the end she triumphed over those three steps, and I believe she willed her sight to improve, against what the doctors predicted. She exercised her eyes with the same self-determination, and, against all odds, she did see and walk again.

They all called her relentless, and I guess she was. It made a lasting impression, inspiring me to never doubt the power of motivation and determination. I was too young to understand all the big words, but she vanquished her devils and would not take "no" or "you can't" for an answer. "Persistence pays off" is what she used to tell us, and I believe it to this day.

Many situations like that have molded my life. The old saying "It's not what happens to you in life, it's how you accept it" has always motivated me when things got tough. You can dwell on what might have been. Instead, it's better to ask, what do I do about it when life gives me a lemon? Hopefully, at that point you remember the old lemonade trick.

The pioneers who trekked from coast to coast in covered wagons encountered hardships that even I wonder how they endured. The Donner Party lost many lives trying to find the way across the Sierra Nevadas, and the Pony Express riders who blazed new trails had challenges in their lives that I can hardly imagine.

I was easily inspired when I was in the navy marching to "Anchors Aweigh." It made me want to be the best sailor I could be. Every time I got bucked off a horse—and there were many—motivation and determination made me want to get up and keep trying until I could ride him. As an aside, it always helped if someone was watching so I wouldn't give up or give in. Getting up the first time isn't so easy, but after several tries, motivation takes over and you look to conquer. Of course, a little luck also never hurt.

Act, Don't React

I learned that to be successful, winners act, participate, stay current and on top of any situation, and help
write the rules they play by. Even a horse senses who
is in control or who is merely a passenger. Consistent
winners in the show arena are those who act, not react.
They have the ability to know in advance how to show
a particular horse in a particular class at a particular show
in front of a particular judge. The blue ribbon usually
goes to the one who acts, and the reactors divide what's
left over.

Because of Frosty's work doing commercials for
Black Bart Motors, I was hired to do a reenactment of
the Pony Express run between Sacramento, California,
and Reno, Nevada. I was to ride the horse to the post
office in town, dismount, and run in. An actor dressed
like me would come out, give a speech to the crowd, and
then go back into the post office. I would then run out
(like a double in the movies), do a flying Pony Express
mount, and gallop out of town with the mailbags. At

one stop, after our usual routine, the actor, instead of returning to the post office, decided to ride out of town himself (he had been drinking). He struggled to get on the horse and kicked him to go forward. Because we had taught the horse many reverse cues, the horse started to back up. The harder the actor kicked, the faster the horse would back. Seeing that it was going to be a disaster, I ran out the door yelling, "Imposter, imposter," pulled the actor from the horse, did the flying mount, and galloped out of town. The scene was saved, the mail was delivered, and the sheriff (who caught on real fast) took the actor away. The horse reacted, I acted, and all ended well.

I always marvel at the Hollywood stuntmen who leap at the chance when the director yells, "Action!" Some get hurt, but very few. When it comes to training horses, I believe in the saying "Never let a horse know what he can't do." I've seen time and again that those who act are also creative and innovative. For instance, roper Glen Franklin started the trend in rodeo's tie-down roping of getting off on the right-hand side instead of the left and going under the rope. This shaved seconds from his time, leading to a whole new way of achieving his goal.

Most competitors don't like to draw first position, but I always felt the opposite. I like to set the bar. In

jumping classes, the first to go has the best footing—
it's been freshly worked; no others have dug it up. You
have an advantage in reining on fresh footing: you don't
have to avoid hazards, like holes from other horses stopping in the same place. In rail classes, the first horse in
the gate sets the pace and the trend for the class. When
judging with others, I wanted to march in first and pick
the best spot so I could see the entire arena.

Being last to do something can also be a plus.
You can size up the class and act in a way that is a little
different from the rest, instead of reacting to what's gone
on before. It really doesn't have to be an emergency
situation in order to act and not react.

One of the best examples of taking charge of a
situation was at a judge's seminar. After several speakers,
most participants were restless, looking at their watches
and generally losing interest (it was mandatory to attend
to keep their licenses). Most felt they knew as much as
the instructor anyway. The next speaker came through
the door dragging a chair. He walked around the room
dragging the chair and not saying a word. After a while
he walked over to the door and threw the chair outside.
There was dead silence; all eyes were on the speaker
and each mind was wondering what the h--- was going
on. He walked to the podium, stopped, turned to the

audience, and said, "If you really want to get something out of this, leave all your baggage outside." You could have heard a pin drop for the rest of his presentation. He most certainly took charge.

One time we were late to pick up Frosty before his TV show. In those days all the shows were done live. This particular show was to be about how we taught Frosty to dance. Arriving at the barn in a dither, we discovered Frosty was not in his stall—and none of the other twenty horses were in theirs either. He had let them all out! It was just getting daylight, and all we could see were silhouettes of horses grazing off in the distance. We corralled all the horses—that is, except Frosty, who decided now was the time for hide and seek. Trying everything from grain to cursing, we finally cornered and loaded him into the trailer and arrived with fifteen minutes to spare.

Upon unloading the horse, we found him limping. "Oh, no! He's lame," I uttered in dismay. I picked up his left front foot, and there in the frog was a rusty nail buried about halfway in. What now? We couldn't go on live television and do a dance act with a lame horse. The director was now yelling, "Five minutes!" As time was ticking, I came up with a solution. "Let's do the whole show around Frosty being hurt. We'll call the vet and have him treat the horse right on the show, and by the end he'll be all right."

It was quite an opening scene. Everyone saw a crowd around Frosty, no one in costume or makeup (although someone had managed to put on Frosty's mask). Having not rehearsed anything like this that week, we had to ad-lib. I started the show by talking about safety, going barefoot and playing where you shouldn't, while casting a side glance or two at the horse. I informed all the viewers how Frosty got hurt. A phone was brought out to call the vet, and I asked Frosty if he wanted to tell the vet what happened, but he shook his head no. I then asked him if he wanted me to tell the vet, and he nodded his head yes.

The veterinarian arrived shortly and treatment was started. After examining the foot, he gave Frosty a tetanus shot and then told us to soak the foot in a bucket of hot water containing Epsom salts. By the end of the program, he should be well. We followed the doctor's instructions and proceeded with our normal routine of having Frosty read the funny paper, do some yes and no tricks, watch some cartoons, and play games with guests from the audience. Frosty stood there the entire time with his foot in the bucket; the vet would check his pulse and the water temperature to make sure he was comfortable.

As the program drew to a close, it was time to show that Frosty was all right. The vet came out and started to lift his foot out of the bucket, but Frosty wouldn't let him pick it up. The vet, not being an actor, got embarrassed and called me over to try … no luck. We both pulled and tugged, but Frosty just put more weight on his foot. More people came to help, without success. We went off the air like a Keystone Kops act. When the red light on the camera went off, signaling we were off the air, Frosty simply lifted his foot out of the bucket and walked off the set! He was definitely in charge.

In the old days, when I was in search of a bargain at the tack shop, I'd work my way through saddles and bridles to the coffee area. There, I would usually find my friend Slim, who over the years had filled my head with commonsense wisdom that I took to heart, perched on his ever-present barrel. On one such occasion, he leaned back, put his feet up (the hole in his right boot seemed larger to me than before), pushed his weathered hat back, and proclaimed, "Somethin's been botherin' me since you was here last."

"Oh, what is it?" I asked.

"All this talk about perception. Don't know what it means to you, but to me it's when somebody else thinks they know what you're thinkin' about. People today are

awful skeptical about judges, trainers, vets … mostly because of gossip or perception."

He went on about the competitions being tougher,
with more interest in judges' methods. Exhibitors are
more aware of different preferences, where one judge
may place more emphasis on way of going and another
on conformation. It doesn't make either of them wrong,
just good or bad, depending on the perception of the
exhibitor.

He hardly took a breath as he lectured me about
judges having different lists of priorities and attaching
importance to different areas. "It might be action, limbs,
feet, or ride, but it's only after ya stand holdin' yer pen in
the center of the ring that ya can appreciate some of the
results that seem strange from ringside."

In my mind, I marveled at how articulate old Slim
had become; his dissertation on perception rivaled that
of Oliver Wendell Holmes. However, wondering how
he had become such an expert on the subject, I had to
ask the obvious question. "Have you ever judged a show,
Slim?"

"Heck yeah, Don. I was really in the cow business
at the time, but they needed a judge, so I was picked out.
Well, I placed horses all day long … done good too, I
thought, when at the end this here woman was waitin'

fer me at the gate. Seems like her horse had placed down the line in several classes. She informed me that this horse had won all over the country, and she thought I shoulda liked him.

"She kept talkin' ... didn't really want to listen to what I had to say. Toward the end of the one-sided conversation, she told me I wasn't fit to judge even cattle. My reply was responding to the matter of perception. I told her if I had been judging cattle that day, her horse woulda certainly been my champion."

I never wanted to underestimate old Slim, as I knew he had done about everything in his day: rodeoed, drove cattle, showed, and apparently even judged. Slim strolled to the stove, offering his seat to me, and I carried on with my own stories of perception.

I recalled one of my stints as officer-of-the-day at the yacht club, a duty that popped up about once a year. My wife and I happened to have taken up sailing when we weren't at horse shows. We had a thirty-foot sloop named *The Idle Cowboy*, which my wife piloted while I handled the sails. The job of the O.D. was to man the radio, take the flags down, and give a howdy to those who came in and a wave to those who left. I shed my big hat and boots and donned a blue blazer, white pants, and Top-Siders. My first duty as O.D. was on a

"Wet Wednesday," from 5:00 PM to 10:00 PM. I'd heard the term associated with sailboat racing, which I knew nothing about.

As I was waiting for the participants to come in and head for the brew and grub, the first captain yanked the door open, marched straight for me, and said, "What are you going to do about the guy who won? He dragged a line at the start, and the one they gave second to missed a buoy."

I stood up, looked him in the eye, and said, "I guess you want to file a protest?" "Yeah!" he said, adding, "How do I do that?"

Just then the next skipper arrived in much the same mood. "Dragged a line," he kept repeating. "Those judges saw him drag a line."

Now I could figure out that missing a buoy was like missing a cone in Western riding, but dragging a line—I didn't have a clue what they were talking about. We sail for pleasure and have never been close to a race except by accident. (I had thought they were being friendly, only to discover they were frantically trying to wave us off their course.)

I was definitely in over my head. But not letting things get the best of me, I said, "Let me find the protest forms." I shuffled papers, opened and closed drawers, to no avail. Several more folks came in grumbling and complaining. I thought sailing was supposed to be fun. I needed time to sort it out, so I sent them all topside for a beer.

I found nothing that even resembled a protest form, but then I knew my luck had changed ... the commodore and vice-commodore of the club came in from an adjoining meeting room, and I came up with a brilliant solution. I appointed them to be a hearing committee, after convincing them this was standard procedure. I later found out no one had ever done this before. I summoned the protestors and proceeded to settle the matter as each testimony was presented to the hearing committee.

Much to my surprise, by the end everyone was in accord; some even shook my hand and told me it was good to have an O.D. who understood and was a "real sailor." Sometimes, perception isn't always reality.

TIGERS AND BOY SCOUTS

When I say "act, don't react," I don't mean charge ahead like a bull with his eyes closed. Rather, be like Davy Crockett, who said, "Be sure you're right, then go ahead," or Confucius, who wrote, "Before the tiger leaps, he takes two steps back." Think it through; be ready; don't hesitate; go for it even though others may disagree at the time. If you have the courage of your convictions, let nothing deter you from pursuing your dream. Today's athletes spend as much time mentally preparing as they do physically preparing. Don't be afraid to raise your hand in class; be the first to volunteer. Follow the Boy Scout motto: "Be prepared."

I've watched heroes take charge even when the odds are long. Remember the 9/11 firefighters and policemen, who, along with average citizens, rushed in regardless of the danger. When the brave men on the diverted flight took over, they knew they would crash, but in doing so they saved many other lives.

Plateaus of Life:
Learn, Do, Teach,
Record

To me, life is a story. How you tell it is what counts. I liken the horse business to plateaus, moving from one to the next, like the four seasons. You continue your activities, but in different ways. You start with learning when you're young, absorbing all the knowledge you can. While still learning, you progress to the doing phase as the active participant, the athlete, the competitor. Next comes the teaching level, passing on to others what you've learned and accomplished. The final recording phase focuses on scrapbooks and writing, preserving memories and deeds for future generations.

When I had nearly completed the learning plateau, I decided I was ready for the active one. I had a stock horse who I thought was pretty handy—could change leads whenever asked, run and slide as fast and as far as I wanted, and turn on a dime. I decided to get my feet wet and entered him in a big show (I wanted to show off my talent). I was warming up in the morning along with the great pros of the day, probably over-doing it a bit. I asked the legendary stock horse trainer M. R. Valdez what he thought of my sliding and turning. "Well, son," he said. "Looks pretty good, but when you can get him to turn away from the fence as well as you have him turning into the fence, you may be ready." Sure enough, the pattern for the class called for turning away from the fence. I was last. Even though plateaus change—learn, do, teach, record—each one carries over to the next. As Jimmy Williams said, "We don't stop playing because we grow old, we grow old because we stop playing."

I'm not sure where desire comes from, but my life had to include horses in some way. I dreamed of being a world champion rodeo cowboy, but after giving it a try, the ground became harder to hit even at that time in my life. Being a famous jockey also crossed my mind, so I galloped horses and rode a few races. But heredity caught up with me, as I grew and gained weight. When I finally took stock, I decided all the learning I had from my father and grandfather would not go to waste if I became either a veterinarian or a horse trainer. As different as my choices were, I knew the academic attraction was not nearly as strong as my horse-trainer aspirations. So I took the plunge to the next plateau, the doing phase.

I paid my dues, working with other trainers and riding bad horses, which I had done frequently growing up. I found I liked the success that blue ribbons brought and compared it to a form of show business. It was more like Broadway than movies because you won or lost and got boos or praise after each performance. Winning was always better.

However, winning without a lot of firsthand experience on horseback will not get the job done. Until you have a leg on each side and your mind in the middle, there is no shortcut or gimmick that will ultimately replace the proper training needed to sustain a horse in the winner's circle. What really produces success, after all else is sifted and sorted, are hours of thought and lots of wet saddle blankets. Pressure is sometimes put upon trainers by owners who are in a hurry to get in the ribbons, one such owner, who had bought a high-priced two-year-old, was pacing the shed row anxiously awaiting a leading trainer's opinion as he looked the horse over. The owner finally asked, "Well, what can you do with him in thirty days?" The trainer scratched his chin, walked around the horse a few more times, and said, "I might learn his name."

There are many devices and gimmicks that could never train a horse, and I have been privy to their use by some so-called trainers during my tenure of teaching. One time I made it a point to stop at the farm of a newcomer to the horse-training ranks. He welcomed me with smiles, a handshake, and a "glad you stopped by." Eager to show me around, his chest swelled as he pointed to his sign out in front. "Designed by the best ad agency in the city," he boasted as we walked. I asked him where he got his training experience. "Oh, I won a few here; a couple there ... decided, since I kept beating my teacher, to go it on my own. See my new truck and matching trailer? It's logoed and lettered by the same agency," he gushed. "Purdy," I quipped.

As we started the tour, I could see the barn was well laid-out, clean and neat, but it had the air of not much use or activity, even though half of the twenty stalls were filled. The horses looked fit and well groomed as he spieled off their pedigrees. The arena was well mani-cured—and empty, even though it was training time in most establishments. The bull pen, hot walker, and turnout paddocks were all sterile too.

He motioned me toward his pride and joy, his eyes sparkling as he opened the door guarding his trade secrets. It was filled with more mechanical devices than I had ever seen. No wonder everything looked so underused; my tour guide was a horse mechanic, not a trainer. He had more contraptions and paraphernalia—even the lab was fully stocked with a cosmetic kit for every horse. There was actually a chart on the wall that had a huge diagram of a horse shaded to show what could be accomplished (without training).

Our tour wound up in the lounge, designed for maximum comfort and horse selling. It had a video library about each horse, along with a well-stocked bar. I took the drink he poured and sat next to the trophy case; most of the accumulated silver was dated well before my host knew if a horse went up a tree or down a hole at night. As we visited, I tried to engage him in some actual training theory. I opened my remarks with, "Boy, I'm impressed. You've got every gadget and gimmick known to man. But whatever happened to plain old wet saddle blankets?" Luckily my intuition had prepared me for his answer. He replied quite matter-of-factly, "Oh, I forgot to show you the laundry room with all my heavy-duty machines … we do all of our own." Good horse trainers have used the wet saddle blanket cliché as long as I can remember to describe how much you work a horse and the time and energy it takes to get one trained. But to my newfound genius, it meant nothing.

We finished our conversation; I thanked him for the drink and the tour. "Most enlightening," were my exact words, as he closed my car door. I looked back at the "Horse Training" sign as I turned onto the road and thought about a few other signs in front of farms that should also have said "Horse Mechanic."

The horse business at that time had grown so rapidly that opportunities knocked on our doors. Specialists were created and the floodgates opened, and those who could win or had won opted for what they thought was the glamorous life of a horse trainer. Classes got bigger and new faces took over. Other methods replaced time. Shortcuts or gimmicks replaced saddle or ground time. Other things became more important—buy, sell, promote. Schooling became secondary.

Having swapped tales and trade secrets with great horsemen in nearly every country, I look back on some of the training philosophies that remain constant over the years, such as "think soft" and "prepare the mind." As we demand more from and put more strain on horses physically, an increased sensitivity regarding their mental well-being should follow. They must be taught from the very beginning that there's a time to relax and a time to soften. It's this type of basic physical and mental conditioning—not the oft-tried gimmicks—that ultimately equips a horse for any task. For a horse to be fit, have plenty of air, and to move up and down the ladder, peaking at a given time, takes hours and thought to accomplish, not just another workbench shortcut. I learned that, just as in life, the pendulum usually swings back to correct itself, usually when one's ego needs deflating.

During my period of blue-ribbon winning, I found communication was another prime element. How can one person understand another or one animal understand the other, or any combination of the two, unless they communicate in some fashion? An old movie titled *My Brother Talks to Horses* is a perfect example. Throughout the horse industry, there are those who talk to horses and there are those to whom horses talk. While at the height of my training career, I had an experience that made me a firm believer in ESP.

It all started with a phone call from a lady who had a horse she wanted me to train. I had a couple of empty stalls and told her to come out any time. A week went by, and one afternoon a brand new pink and black Cadillac with matching trailer (all the rage then) pulled into the yard. A statuesque lady emerged in expensive riding clothes and asked where she might find Mr. Burt. "That's me," I quipped. "What can I do for you?"

She introduced herself and asked me to follow her to the trailer. Without assistance, she unloaded the horse, walked it a few feet away, and began talking to the mare. Motioning me over, she said, "Mr. Burt, I would like you to meet Prissy Pandora. Prissy, this is Mr. Burt." The mare and I stood and looked at each other, which I thought was ridiculous. She then led the mare away and had another one-sided conversation. Returning, she said, "Prissy likes you but she doesn't want to stay here."

She told me the horse was entered in the Grand National at the Cow Palace, which was just three weeks away, and she had just been hauled down from Alaska last week. She assured me the mare was properly trained, having been ridden on the runway while air force jets were taking off and landing, until (I found out later) the pilots had her ruled off the field. She showed me photos of the horse being transported, loose, in a pickup truck bed with no sides, which added to my skepticism.

To appease her, I said, "Before we make any commitments, let me ride her and evaluate her potential as a trail horse and her chances of winning." She agreed and saddled the horse, all the while carrying on a conversation (not with me). I rode the mare awhile and then tried some obstacles. As I approached a row of six tires, Prissy reared up and jumped away. After disciplining her, I tried again, no luck. The same scenario was displayed at the bridge, gate, and back-thru. Riding over to the owner, I said, "Ma'am, there isn't a prayer in the world I can get her ready in three months, let alone three weeks, for any show."

"Just a moment please, Mr. Burt," she said, and she proceeded to shake her finger at the mare. "Prissy," she began, "you don't have to stay here if you don't want to, but I want Mr. Burt to ride you in the show. And if you're not good I won't let you eat grass with Aquillo for a week." (Aquillo, I learned, was the mare's two-year-old colt.)

"Now, Mr. Burt, please try her again."

I climbed back on and we miraculously proceeded through the course with nary a foot out of place. I was dumbfounded. She patted Prissy and said to me, "I'm sorry she was so naughty." In jest, I told her, "Lady, you don't need me to show her. You seem to already have the magic touch." But she still insisted.

We finally struck a deal I couldn't refuse. She paid me a lot of money and brought the horse every day. After the training sessions, some good, some bad, I doubted our chances of winning anything.

There were about fifty head in the trail horse sweepstakes, corralled in a holding area so we couldn't school before the class. Those were the days before you were able to see the course ahead of time, much less walk it. While the judge described the route and obstacles, I felt a tug on my chaps. My ever-present owner handed me a package, which turned out to be an air force survival kit, K-rations and all. "Thought you might need this," she said. "It may be a long morning." The lady was dead serious.

Being fortieth on the list, I did have a long wait, and periodically Prissy's owner would come by for a few words with her. Seems my high-toned lady would check out an obstacle, see how others did it, and return to tell Prissy what was going on.

Finally it was my turn, and my companion disappeared (I thought). We were about three feet from the first obstacle (a bridge, covered with greenery and flowers, placed on a 4x4 so it would teeter), when a clear, rather lyrical voice sang the tune "My Wonderful, Wonderful One." It was my owner! How embarrassing! I wanted to die, but I stayed focused and continued perfectly over the first obstacle. As I trotted to the next obstacle, my sing-along followed me around in the moat that encircled the arena. I loped to the next one, thinking I could escape her, but she was a tall lady with a big stride. Prissy was being letter-perfect. It was hard to believe.

After we finished the course to a round of applause, the owner met me in the holding pen. I practically yelled, "What were you doing?" She informed me that as Prissy was going to the first obstacle, she appeared a little nervous. "When I sing her favorite song, she settles down and does her best." I not only ended up with the blue ribbon, money, trophy, and saddle, but a true story that I'll never forget.

Something definitely passed between her and the horse—a look, an attitude, a sound—that allowed their vibes to correspond. This sixth sense, verbalized or not, is often evident not only in the horse business but in every phase of life.

I once knew of a horse that had been sent to many trainers for schooling. This particular horse had it all—class, ability, style—but there was one problem. The horse was a sweetheart at home, but the moment the gate closed at the show, he turned into the Terminator. He could stop faster at a jump than any horse I'd ever seen.

A young and eager horse trainer (who, of course, didn't have any money) prevailed upon his customers

to buy the horse. Having faith and trust in their trainer's judgment, as most good customers do, they bought
him. The horse's bad habits kept sending the trainer end
over end, crashing through the jump, no matter what
schooling methods he tried. The owners were disheart-
ened and ready to sell.

The young and eager trainer, however, was not
the sort to give up easily, even though this happened
over and over again. Then one day while schooling, the
horse fell, and both rider and horse found themselves in
a situation where they had to rely on each other for help
in order to get out of the spot they were in. At that moment, communication in the form of confidence passed
between them; a touch, a word, a sign compelled each
to help the other.

The crisis passed, but after that incident there
was a definite change in the attitude of both horse and
trainer. Confidence began to develop; thought and
understanding were taking place. The horse from that
day forth won class after class and went on to become
one of the greatest champions I've ever known in the
show ring. Whatever the horse or trainer lacked before,
the missing link had been found. The communication
that developed between them was what was needed to
achieve success.

The great horsemen have all discovered the secret of communication. However, the ability to communicate often requires more listening than talking. Maybe that's why we were born with two ears and only one mouth.

Necessity might be the mother of invention, but adversity is what changed my life forever. While laid up, I was solicited by my peers to judge a few horse shows. They thought as long as I wasn't competing against them, it would be fair for me to judge. This not only rewarded me with a livelihood but helped the transition into my teaching phase. Teaching, I found, is not simply giving lessons to others. It is done through many mediums, even during the doing plateau. You actually do a lot of teaching by example. Many times you stumble onto something completely new and innovative by mistake.

While judging in my cast, unable to walk far, I would step just inside the in-gate and view the class from that vantage point instead of from the center of the arena. It was amazing how much more I could see—not only coming, going, and broadside, but the whole class. I prided myself on not missing much in the arena, and judging from this stance gave me the advantage in rail classes. Over-fence and reining classes were much better viewed from a raised platform outside the arena. These positions are still in use today.

You can never completely disregard the previous plateaus, even into the final phase. As we climb to the recording plateau, we must carry all of our previous experiences with us up the mountain (not an easy task), and oftentimes we fall along the way. Because of age or physical limitations, many never make it and don't record all the things that got them that far. The photos we keep, the scrapbooks and letters dating to our youth, and our achievements all contribute to this phase. I don't mean writing books or stories for others to read but recording for one's self and family.

Regrets also accompany the recording phase, where the area is smaller. We don't have to share all of our ups and downs. However, do record them in your mind and relive them in your thoughts when you are all alone, which is often enough. It would be fantastic if everyone would record their memories and experiences in writing. What a history book that would make!

Every Horse, Every Person, Has a Place

In training horses, one of the most emphasized practices my grandfather passed down to me—and I repeat it often—was, "The horse will tell you everything, if you take the time to pay attention." I'm reminded of the story of a reining horse I had in training that was once Wild Bill Elliott's rearing horse for rodeo appearances. He was a mediocre reining horse and took a lot of figuring out. He was turned out in a round pen with six-foot-high solid walls when a fire engine went by with its siren blaring. Frightened, the horse stood flat-footed and jumped out without touching the sides. Three weeks later, after schooling him to be a jumper, he won his first championship and then became champion at the Cow Palace (the West's largest show), as well as a Pacific Coast champion several times. That's what he wanted to be.

Another parallel story is about the trick horse I had on television in Las Vegas. He rode in elevators, went up and down stairs in casinos with hundreds of people, and was put in all sorts of peculiar situations. To me, it was only natural that he also could be a champion trail horse at the shows. At that particular time, there was a trail horse extravaganza held at the Del Mar Fairgrounds. Naturally I entered him, because he had been subjected to more obstacles than any trail horse–course designer could dream up. Practice? Why, I thought, nothing could possibly bother him; besides, he was too busy performing.

The big day came. The course was laid out with many of the standard obstacles: walk-overs, a bridge, a mailbox, back-thrus, etc. There were a few traps laid here and there: dry ice, water, chickens in a coop, a clothesline to go under, and various other so-called audience-pleasing lures. I was not concerned; my horse was infallible. We lined up and were given instructions by the designer and the judge. As I watched several of the horses ahead of me do pretty well, I still had all the confidence in the world. This would be a piece of cake. We entered the arena. He spooked at the mailbox, fell off the bridge, scattered the walk-over poles, and refused to back up. As we finished the course, I looked back at total devastation. Not one obstacle was left intact. I could sense the crowd chuckling, as I had bragged long and hard about my super-horse. I rode up to the judge, who also was snickering, tipped my hat, and asked my horse to bow. Doing so without hesitation, he generated instant applause from the audience. My horse was a ham and wanted to perform tricks, not be a show horse.

Most people think of the horse business as fun, something they'd like to try. But as life sorts it out, not everyone can be a great rider, trainer, or judge. Talent, physical limitations, and temperament often hinder options. But if one truly has the aspiration, there are many other sidelines of the business that might be of interest: show manager, ringmaster, announcer, course designer, groom, teacher, shoer, hauler. The main thing is to be a success (not only with horses), a principle my dad instilled in me. From breeders to writers and everybody in between, there is a niche in the horse business for most everyone. We have created many new fields that were formerly mostly taken care of by a veterinarian. Now you often hear of acupuncturists, teeth floaters, massagers, psychics, and whisperers; every year a new profession seems to be created out of necessity. There is an old saying, "Find a need and fill it," that exists full force in the horse industry. I can't even begin to list the jobs, positions, or careers that relate to the horse.

I met a girl who all her life wanted to be with horses. She cleaned stalls, groomed, braided, and gave lessons so she could ride. She put her heart and soul into a riding career and started off with a bang. One miscue, a misplaced step, sent her crashing to the ground. She had fallen before but this time was different. She felt nothing from the waist down. Wheelchair-bound, she found she could still teach, buy and sell horses, and oversee a full training operation, which gave her a degree of success and happiness.

She was an avid reader and a student of the horse, and the more she learned, the more her interest was piqued. She had what many call a photographic memory, which enabled her to recite bloodlines and the history of every horse she came in contact with. People started calling her for information and touting her as a walking pedigree encyclopedia. But nothing really satisfied her totally until she went to work for a large breed association. She quickly was promoted from job to job and eventually became the registrar for the breed, creating new methods of identifying, recording, and storing information. She revolutionized the industry and was a tremendous success. When I met her for the first time, she said, "Pardon me, I'm handicapped and can't walk." I told her I hadn't noticed, I thought she was just short. We've been friends life.

Every successful person I know needs and uses what I call a "ground man": someone to observe, confer with, and give advice. I've been fortunate to have had several. I was always a pretty good rider, but it was helpful to have someone watch my horses work and tell me how they were doing, good or bad. Early in my career, I needed even more help and guidance in handling business and the social graces, and two people stood out prominently in this capacity.

When I first opened my training stable, my very first clients were Herb and Babs Bishop. Babs saw right off that I had little or no knowledge of etiquette. I didn't even know why they put two forks on the table. When I was growing up, going out to dinner meant eating at Albins Drug Store. She took on the task of upgrading me, including instruction in when and how to write "thank you" notes. Herb realized from our first conversation that, while I might know about horses, I didn't speak or understand business language. So between the two, they taught me proper decorum and how to run a training business.

One instance that stands out in my mind that included them both was a sit-down dinner at their home.

Some very prominent guests were invited, including the governor, who was being honored. Babs had explained to me about seating arrangements, when to talk, etc. Well, it seems the governor's favorite food was asparagus, which I had never seen before, much less eaten. It was ceremoniously served amongst much conversation about where it came from and how it was prepared. Practicing my newly acquired social graces, I "dug in." Just before the plates were removed, Belle, the maid, came to me and whispered, "Don, you ate the wrong end." Red-faced, I looked around (which I should have done sooner) and saw that everyone else had eaten the spear end, while I had eaten the stem. Herb Bishop, without hesitation, rose to the occasion and simply stated, "I always eat the stem last, it's the best part," and proceeded to eat the stem. The other guests followed his lead, and I sheepishly ate the head. He had bailed me out of a very embarrassing situation.

As time went on, he became a real proponent of teaching me the ropes of business. He was president of the Squirt Company, with a Who's Who list of board members. He made me hand in a written report each month on the status of his horses and shows and any related matters. This led to my appearing at each board meeting and giving an oral report and answering any questions from the members. I had to account for every expenditure and even explain why some of their horses won and some lost. This not only prepared me later in life to be able to address all levels of society but also to field inquiries of all types.

Our relationship lasted until Herb's death. I still look at the old pictures of my first horse van; he was instrumental in guiding me in its purchase. I had to keep an accurate record of its use and make sure it "paid for itself," as he used to insist. People still remember the decals on each side and the rear of the van, which featured their logo and the saying, "Drink Squirt and ride with Burt!"

Not only among trainers of horses but in just about any sport or activity, there are those who simply watch, counsel, and offer a remedy to the situation. Again, I have had the best, who have had no qualms in discussing with me the right or wrong way that I do things. Sometimes it comes pretty near to being a crutch with me, because my mechanical skills are practically nil, or at least my wife thinks so.

One time way back, I was asked to look at a horse for a friend of mine, try it out and evaluate how good it would be for him (something I do well). The barn was about ten miles from my place. Having just purchased a new car, I was anxious to give it a spin. I tried the horse and returned to my car, which was parked in front of the stable office, only to discover I had a flat tire.

No problem, I thought. I opened the rear trunk and stared at the empty space. This particular sports car (a two-seater Fiat X1/9) carried its engine crossways just in front of the rear trunk. It also had a large trunk area in the front. Closing the rear, I opened the front end. Nothing was there either. Perplexed, I went into the office to use the phone, where several people were lounging around drinking coffee.

I called my wife and told her that I had a flat tire and there was no spare or jack, so she'd have to come and get me. "Where did you look?" she asked. "In both trunks," I sort of snapped back, with a where-do-you-think-I-would-look attitude. She merely replied, "If you look behind the passenger seat, you'll find the spare tire and the jack."

After I opened both trunks and then called home, all eyes were on me. I returned to the car and, sure enough, there was the spare and a jack, just as she said. I put the jack together. Kind of a strange-looking one, I thought, just a straight bar with no hook or flange on it to catch the bumper. Oh, well. I placed it under the rear of the car and started to jack up the car. It would get just off the ground, but because the bar had no hook, it would slide off and crash to the ground. I did this a few times before I threw everything in the trunk and asked to use the phone again.

I told my wife that she needed to come and pick me up because the jack was broken and wouldn't work. "How were you using it?" came her question.

"Like you use any jack," I said, quite frustrated. "I put it under the rear bumper and tried to jack it up but there's no hook on the end and the car kept slipping off."

Quite patiently, she advised, "Look under the car on the frame just in front of the flat tire; there should be a little square notch that the rod fits into. The car jacks up from the side so you can change either the front or rear tire." I hung up, ignored my audience, took the stuff from the trunk, found the notch under the side of the car, jacked up the car, changed the tire, and gave my onlookers a thumbs-up as I drove off. This was a brand-new car. How did she learn where everything was so quickly? I then remembered that my wife reads all instructions before attempting to operate or put anything together. It's a good thing!

THE ABCS OF WINNING

A . . . is for ATTITUDE, one of the most important ingredients in every champion. You must have a positive attitude, not a negative one or even sometimes. The consistent winner is the one who can overcome adversity and turn it into success. The right attitude is not "I think I can," but "I know I can."

B . . . is for BASICS, the foundation of every winner. Whatever event you compete in, the groundwork must be laid in order for you to come out on top. Whenever you're in a tough spot or somewhat undecided, always go back to the basics, whether schooling yourself or your horse.

C . . . is for CONDITIONING, an often-overlooked factor in winning. Your horse must be in the finest condition, as well as your tack, and continually maintained. You, too, must be in condition, both physically and mentally, to be in contention for the blue ribbon.

D . . . is for DEDICATION. Champions are not made overnight. If you give up easily, you probably will never reach the top. Your horse must also have dedication, or what is referred to as "heart," to keep trying no matter how long the show season might be.

E . . . is for ENTHUSIASM. Without this element, life becomes routine, or rote. A winner is always enthusiastic about every class he enters and never coasts or lets down, no matter what the competition may be.

F . . . is for FLEXIBILITY, which a true champion must have. He must be able to adapt to any situation to be able to show in many different arenas, facilities, and surroundings in front of many different judges. The ability to adapt is a must.

G . . . is for GOAL, regardless of the type of horse you show. You must have something in front of you to strive for: a peak that makes the climb worthwhile. Don't simply drift in and out of one show after another, but aspire for the blue at the end of the rainbow.

H . . . is for HORSEMANSHIP, a requirement for all classes. Even though many classes are not judged on the rider or handler *PER SE*, you must demonstrate good horsemanship no matter whether you're showing a pleasure horse, a jumper, or a halter competitor. The person who displays horsemanship will easily be recognized by the judge.

I . . . is for INDIVIDUALITY. Every champion is a champion on his own; he finds what he does best and works at it. This also applies to the horse; if your horse wants to be a jumper, why try to show him in the trail horse division? Individuality parallels suitability, you to your horse and, as individuals, to each other.

J . . . is for JUDGES. Without them we wouldn't have horse shows. There are good judges and some who are not so good—just ask around. The winners think their judges are great, and the losers want to leave before the show is over. Just keep in mind that the judges are only hired to follow the technical rules and give his opinion, which may or may not be the same as yours. One thing though—there's always another show next week.

K . . . is for KNOWLEDGE, a much-needed requirement in any walk of life. What happens to most losers is they get a little bit of knowledge and think they know it all. A winner keeps learning something new at every show and puts it to work in his behalf. Learning is a never-ending process where horses are concerned.

L . . . is for LISTENING, a quality that is apparent in winners. You'd be surprised at the number of contestants who do not listen. Consequently when instructions are given, either by the judges or their trainers, they've already lost the class by not knowing what to do. A word to the wise is sufficient — if you're listening, that is.

M . . . is for MANNERS. They will always stand out above the crowd — and lack of manners stands out even more. At a show, there is no reason for a horse to be ill-mannered and cause problems for others. Manners are not limited to the horse, though; they are just as important for the exhibitors. Yes, good or bad manners in parents stand out too.

N . . . is for NEATNESS, an attribute often overlooked. It is a real privilege to be able to show a horse; it is a form of show business. There is no excuse for a lack of neatness or cleanliness for either you or your horse. Your clothes or tack don't have to be expensive, but those in the winner's circle are usually neat and clean.

O . . . is for OBSERVATION. To be a winner, you must be able to observe what's going on around you, in relation to others in the class. Which obstacle is placed where? How can I get on the rail by myself? Where is the best place to slide? Which jump is the hardest for my horse? One of the main attributes of a successful professional is the ability to observe and put those observations to beneficial use.

P . . . is for PROMPTNESS, which is the ability to readily do what is asked, from getting on the proper lead to being able to back up when the judge says, "It's your turn." Promptness goes hand in hand with preparedness, which means getting there on time and being able to get the job done. That's what winners are made of.

Q . . . is for QUESTION. Winners aren't hesitant or embarrassed if they don't understand something. Never be afraid to ask about the routine you are given. If you're having trouble with your horse, don't continue along blindly. If you think for yourself, you'll find you have many questions—if you ask, you will receive.

R . . . is for RULES, which govern the whole horse-show world. Know what they are before you get to the show. Rules change every year. Unless you keep up, you'll be showing today's horse in yesterday's fashion.

S . . . is for SPORTSMANSHIP, another quality that is readily displayed at many horse shows. Good and bad sportsmanship are often evident when winners and losers leave the arena. To win the blue ribbon doesn't necessarily make you a winner—showing respect to others counts. In

this sport, especially for junior riders, one of the greatest
achievements is to exhibit good sportsmanship.

T . . . is for TRAINING. There are no shortcuts, just wet saddle
blankets. Don't be in a hurry—good training takes time.
The more training you and your horse can acquire, the more
ribbons will hang on your wall. Training comes in many forms
and on several levels, from beginning to advanced. So opt for
the best match for you and your horse.

U . . . is for the UNSTYLE. I've written many times about the
unstyle. All riders and horses do not come with the same size,
shape, or ability. So you must rely on the relationship of form
to function for you and the horse. Find whatever makes you
and your horse look the best. Don't copy someone else—
develop a style all your own.

V . . . is for VERSATILITY, an attribute many have but most
do not use. To really gain from the sport and be a true
winner, you must work on both sides of the fence—showing
and helping behind the scenes. By working with others
to contribute and improve, keeping your horse happy, not
sour or over-faced, you keep yourself sharp and up to the
competition.

W . . . is for WORK. Plain old hard work is the only way to get ahead. Not much more can be said about this—there is no substitute for work.

X . . . is for XENOPHOBIA, which means fear of anything strange or foreign. You should avoid this fear. To be a winner, you must accept change. Don't hesitate to try something new, as long as you've thought it all out beforehand. To quote the old saying: "The turtle never goes anywhere until he sticks his neck out."

Y . . . is for YOURSELF. It is a wise person who truly knows himself, most definitely in the horse business. You need to know your capabilities and limitations. There are differences between trying, being aggressive, and being reckless. Don't fool yourself; find a way you can succeed. Remember, you can't control your horse until you can control yourself.

Z . . . is for ZEALOUSNESS, in your contention for the winner's circle. Be eager to prove yourself in competition. The horse-show business can be very rewarding—tackle it without hesitation.

Passion, Heart, Talent

If you look at the people who have been dominant in their fields, from the beginning the thing that always seems to separate them from the rest is a passion to be great. There can be many motivations, but 99 percent of the time greatness is achieved through passion—by loving what you do. Many have talent and ability but lack heart, which equals dedication. There are many horses that have great talent to run, jump, slide, and spin, but the competitive edge the consistent winners have is heart. Talent and passion need the third ingredient—the heart—to conquer and win regardless of adversity.

Yes, heart is something you can see. It can be likened to staying power: the ability to turn adversity into a blue ribbon or the winner's circle. Heart is a form of attitude; it knows no boundaries. Horses that have a great deal of heart have an aura around them, a presence, that oftentimes covers up some of their physical shortcomings. Heart is what keeps a horse going consistently under all circumstances. Some think that heart comes from physical ability, but I've seen horses do things they really shouldn't be capable of accomplishing. True, the horse's conformation must be properly proportioned for him to be an athlete, but to be a consistent winner, he must have that extra little ingredient.

Years ago I had two jumping horses. One was nearly structurally perfect and, when he wanted to, could "jump the moon," as long as everything went just right. If things didn't click or an adjustment had to be made, he could stand you on your head just as easily.

The other horse, not so physically perfect but a steady trier, would give his all every time and never let you down. He ended up winning more than the better-conformed horse and by a wider margin—sort of the tortoise and hare fable in reality.

Passion can not be taught, I think. There is no way to train and achieve it, like a goal. To me, passion is a quality that comes from deep inside. *My Heroes Have Always Been Cowboys* is a movie I've seen so many times that I can recite the script. Its star is one of my favorite people—Ben Johnson, who played the father in a role made for him because of his background (the movie is set in the Oklahoma area where he grew up). The movie was shown several times recently during the National Finals Rodeo, which harnessed me to the couch for ten days, except for a few nights at the races for the Los Alamitos Champion of Champions.

During that time—maybe because of my new big-screen TV—I became more aware of the competitors' faces and expressions while winning, losing, or just hanging out. It brought back memories of Al Jolson, who turned up all the theater lights so he could "see their faces" while he sang. I discovered that nearly all of the cowboys at the National Finals Rodeo (NFR) showed true passion for what they were doing. It was obvious they not only lived it but loved it. The good horses had that same look of passion and the will to win; they were never complacent. I noticed it at the races; horses, jockeys, and trainers alike were loving what they were doing.

At our old-timer lunch gatherings, attended by more than twenty-five past champions of some sort or other, they still show that passion when reliving the old days. Some of them, mostly stuntmen, like to tell stories about each other hardly being able to get out of the chair. But when the cameras start rolling, the aches and pains miraculously disappear for a short while. Then they hobble back.

During the first couple of rounds of the NFR, the rough stock riders bounced up from the ground and skipped off. By the last few rounds, they could hardly get on, but when the chute opened, pain vanished until the ground was met abruptly. Most, slow to get up, hobbled out of the arena. When they were interviewed, each spoke of their participation with a sense of passion. No wonder they were champions.

A WHOLE LOT OF HEART

I'm often reminded of the story of Snowbound and Bill Steinkraus, who captured the show jumping gold at the Olympics in Mexico City in 1968. Snowbound was a mediocre, unsound racehorse in northern California in the early 1960s. Discovered by John Galvin as a green hunter being shown by Show Jumping Hall of Famer Barbara Worth Oakford, Snowbound was presented as a gift to his daughter, Olympic dressage rider Patricia, and loaned to the United States Equestrian Team (USET) for Steinkraus to ride. Always threatened by a recurrence of the tendon trouble that had driven him from the track, Snowbound was too valuable to the team to risk in ordinary classes and so was shown lightly. In 1968, he jumped double clears in all of the European Nations' Cups in which he competed. At the Olympics, he jumped one of only two clear rounds in the first round of the individual competition, and though he finished on three legs, he incurred only a single fault over the huge fences of the second round to win the gold with Steinkraus aboard. That shows not only passion and talent, but a whole lot of heart.

Patience, Persistence, Sacrifice

The life of one of history's truly great individuals sums up his character. He failed in business back in 1831. He was defeated for the legislature in 1832. He failed in business again in 1833 and was elected to the legislature in 1834. His sweetheart died in 1835, and he had a nervous breakdown in 1836. He was defeated for speaker of the house in 1838 and defeated for land officer and congressman in 1843. He was elected to Congress in 1846, defeated for vice president in 1856, and defeated for senator in 1858. Even though many times he wanted to quit, he didn't. He was elected president in 1860. He never gave up. His name was Abraham Lincoln—and the rest is a story told over and over.

Seabiscuit was a rough-hewn, undersized horse with knees that wouldn't straighten all the way. He fought his trainers and floundered at the lowest level of racing until his dormant talent was discovered by three men. Charles Howard, a former bicycle repairman who made a fortune by introducing the automobile to the American West, bought him for a pittance and entrusted him to Red Pollard, a failing jockey, and Tom Smith, "The Lone Plainsman," who carried generations of lost wisdom about the secrets of horses. From 1936 to 1940, Seabiscuit endured a remarkable run of bad fortune, conspiracy, and injury to establish himself as one of history's most extraordinary athletes. He had lickety-split speed, versatility, and indomitable will; he shipped thousands of railroad miles, carried staggering weight to victory against the best horses in the country, and shattered more than a dozen track records. His rivalry with Triple Crown–winner War Admiral terminated in a spectacular match race that is still widely regarded as the greatest horse race ever run. His trouble-plagued four-year quest to conquer the world's richest horse race became one of the most legendary struggles in sports.

Patience is a lost virtue, many have said, but it does pay off in the end. When young, I wanted everything right now. As I grew a little older, tomorrow sufficed. Then came the realization that all good things come to those who wait. Have patience—all things are difficult before they become easy. Along with patience comes persistence. Waiting doesn't mean you give up or quit trying.

I had a horse sent to me who was a notorious stopper at fences. He'd stop and throw his rider off in nearly every class. He would school at home like a champion, but in the show ring it was a different story. After being stood on my head numerous times in front of my peers, I vowed not to give up. I took him to shows way out in the boondocks and persuaded them to let me set a course and school after the show. I hauled jumps around for months trying to discover his secret. Through trial and error, I stumbled onto the fact that he jumped okay from the right lead and never stopped when courses went to the right. Most courses at the larger shows began to the left, which was my ticket for a fall.

I started talking with course designers to try to persuade them to go to the right. The first time they did so, there was a massive uprising from the other exhibitors. It was probably due to the fact I won the class with no stops. The horse had all the jumping talent in the world, but somewhere along the line he had learned to drop his left shoulder and duck out or stop at the last stride. I had my wife film his every movement going around the course both ways. I discovered after many bruises that he would put his left ear back dramatically just before he was going to quit. I also found through study that if I touched him with my spur on his right side, his left ear would go forward and he would raise his left shoulder. Sounds a bit technical, but patience and persistence paid off. When on course, all I had to do was time everything perfectly when going to the left. It kind of became a ritual after awhile: approach the jump, left ear cocked back, spur on right side, left ear went forward, and he jumped in stride and clean. I went on to win the Pacific Coast Working Hunter championship several times, as long as my timing was in sync with his.

I never shared my secret with others—I should have, but I was protecting my turf, I thought. I had to sacrifice many classes along the way in the learning process and probably thought I was justified at the time. Seems when I was young, sacrifice was the order of the day. During the Depression years, just to eat regularly meant a sacrifice of some sort. Growing up with my invalid mother during the war, sacrifice was a part of life. In fact, I really didn't know that I was sacrificing because I couldn't distinguish what I might be missing. I guess it taught me how to appreciate all the good things I had and develop a talent and desire to use it. I had horses to ride, which not only brought a business but a way of life. So my clothes were a little old and worn and my boots had holes in the soles—as long as I could pay the entry fee, the horse show world was mine.

There was gas rationing during the war years, which left none for hauling horses. A group would get together and each would ride one horse and lead two, leaving at midnight to get to a show that was several hours away. We'd show all day and ride back. Funny thing, through all that sacrifice, our horses stayed pretty fit, and so did we. Later, when we could travel hundreds of miles, most show arenas didn't have stalls, so we made do by tying our horses to trees, trailers, or anything else available. Now, we're all pretty spoiled with air-conditioned vans and drivers to haul the horses and grooms to do the preparations so we can stay clean and dressed; some even strut around and survey their setup. Hotel rooms to sleep in have replaced the stalls we used when I was young. But I sometimes wonder if the stars of today missed something by bypassing the struggles that required patience, persistence, and, most of all, sacrifice, which was the great teacher of the past.

Even though she was dealt adversity in her life, Pamela Carruthers always managed to have another door open, giving her the opportunity to excel in a profession mainly dominated by men. She is retired now but has led an ever-eventful life spent climbing from one plateau to another.

In 1979, clutching an envelope filled with hundred-pound notes and a ticket to London, she was secretly escorted, cloak-and-dagger style, through the countryside to catch the last flight out of Tehran during the stormy uprising in Iran, just days before the Shah escaped. This scene of intrigue etched a memory or two for Pamela to relate to her grandchildren.

Pamela had been the guest of the Royal Iranian Horse Society, of which the Shah was president, to design the courses for a big international horse show. Security surrounding the Shah was so tight that when she was introduced, three bulletproof glass doors had to open and close before she could shake his hand. His entrance and departure were entirely by helicopter; he never rode in a car. She was aware the banks had been closed all week and was worried about getting the money that was owed to her. When the British Embassy, along with the British Airways office, was burned and all communications severed, she forgot about the money and concentrated on saving her life. With the help of friends, her remuneration was mysteriously produced in hundred-pound notes, and she was urgently whisked via back roads to the airport to board the last flight (for civilians) to London. Luckily, she had a ticket, for there were over 4,000 people all trying to flee the country.

Determined to board the flight, she "literally stood on the luggage counter and wouldn't let anyone else get by." She got the last seat on the plane. Once back in England, she realized just how lucky she had been to get back home, much less to have been paid—and in pounds! This was only one of many episodes in her life.

Things have a way of happening to Pamela that might prove disastrous for others, but her honesty, integrity, and sheer tenacity push the positive switch on, miraculously converting things in her favor. Pamela has been a friend of our family forever, it seems, as our home became hers whenever she was stateside, hopscotching around the world designing her vivid signature floral fences at prestigious horse shows. Until a few years ago, she resided in Wiltshire, which is about hundred miles due west of London, not far from Wales, in a sixteenth-century cottage on a six-acre farm. Her expertise stems from her early years, and she likes to tell the story.

"I was born in England during WWI—during the biggest air raid they ever had," she said, holding her ears. "And I've been gun shy ever since. My father was killed in the war when I was three months old. My mother remarried, and we went to India for a while. I learned to ride at the age of five, got my first pony at twelve, and from then on I was completely horse mad. I rode to school, fox hunted; I was always on a horse. When I was fifteen, my mother thought I needed a little polish and less horseplay, so I was sent off to a French finishing school. However, my fervor for horses never waned, and I begged to ride anything, even wild race horses."

Her step-grandmother, in a rash moment, introduced her to the top French riders, which gave her an entrée to ride in the ladies classes in the Paris Horse Show. "I climbed on top of some of the best horses in France; at that time, the French horses were by far the best in the world, and the jumping was much superior to anything we had in England. This was what gave me the taste to eventually become a course designer. But, at that time, I never envisioned myself having to earn my own living."

It's interesting to note that the reason she was sent to France really had no affect on her later life but, oddly enough, provided her with a way of supporting herself, as she has been doing the last thirty-plus years. Having married at the beginning of World War II, she had two children and a farm to look after, so riding had to take a backseat. "I did have an ex–race horse, which we hitched up to a dog cart and used for transportation … not much traffic on the roads because there wasn't any gas."

After the war she started showing horses, and she jumped with the British team on a horse called Galway Bay. The fact that they didn't allow women in the Nation's Cup was the reason she finally sold her horse. "He was too good of a horse not to have the chance to prove himself." Shortly after that, her marriage failed, leaving her with no money and two children to raise. This curtailed her activities for a while, as she had to earn a living and give her children an education. "I took other people's horses to break and train and went to some of the smaller local shows, where I found the courses were so bad I couldn't bear it. So I started designing my own. After doing this for a couple of years, I was extremely lucky, because Hickstead was just starting up, and I became the assistant course designer. I quickly advanced and have been their chief course designer for over twenty-five years. I couldn't have had a better place to learn my trade, as I had beautiful grounds and unlimited material, and the best riders in the world came to show their horses.

"From there I progressed to other European countries and on across the Atlantic and worked my way from the East Coast to the West Coast and into Canada. It's a terrific challenge to build courses that will improve the horses and riders, and this is fundamentally my goal when I go to new places. I don't think people realize the work that's involved in the preparation of a course. I grew up with television at home, where they require your plans be drawn at least three weeks in advance. I do all my plans ahead of time on graph paper, with ample copies.

"Occasionally," Pamela fessed up, "I do make a mistake. However, I always go up to the riders afterwards and apologize, and we discuss the reason why it happened. At one show I had a red fence (colored red rails over a ditch) and had used it in a small class towards the end of the course without it causing any problem. As it was the second fence in the big class, I didn't raise it any higher. But it kept being knocked down with monotonous regularity, and I couldn't understand it. After I went and stood behind it, I could see why—there were two red cars directly in line; the red rails just disappeared into the red of the cars. I don't think people consider these things or the position of the sun. Jumping a water jump going directly into the sun is quite difficult. White rails over liverpools are equally as hard—they take on a shimmering quality which gives an unusual illusion. Actually the degree of difficulty has less to do with the route and more to do with color, type, distance, and placement of the fences."

You could always spot Pamela in her own private golf cart, her graph charts and tape measure in tow, chugging around the course administering to her ring crew like a master drill sergeant. Her wish was their command, and her reputation for perfection and detail was revered by all. She has had her name commingled with the noteworthiest of the famous. During the 1984 Olympics, a party at the Los Angeles Equestrian Center was held in her honor and an arena dedicated in her name by HRH. Prince Philip. And, I might add, it isn't just anyone who can pick up the phone when in a bind and have HRH. Prince Philip fly you the needed materials, but that's what Pamela did one time when she was in Venezuela.

Because of her love for horses, she has dedicated her career to the betterment of the sport of show jumping. She often provided commentary for the BBC when not designing courses, and she enjoyed Wimbledon from the royal box. She was the easiest houseguest in the world because she made herself right at home. During her stay, my wife and I found ourselves pronouncing English words properly and learned that asparagus is the only vegetable that the British eat with their fingers. We always respected her aversion to the shortened American version of her name, and we never offered her a spot of tea.

Attitude

During a judging career that spanned some forty years, I saw just about all forms of attitude. As Wayne Newton once said, "There are good shows and there are bad shows, good audiences and bad ones. You just hope the bad performances and bad audiences don't show up on the same night."

Attitude is reflected in everything we do: how we treat others, approach a problem, or figure out a horse, whose attitude can change from lesson to lesson. My dad always said before we turned in at night, "Don't get up on the wrong side of the bed in the morning." Attitude is one of a person's most visible traits. It's like wearing your heart on your sleeve. Cocky, sullen, hesitant, and even fearful— they all stand out like a watermelon in a bunch of grapes. A winning attitude must be positive—not "I think I can," but "I know I can."

Your attitude on a given day is reflected in how you train, judge, or just make it through the day. Sometimes you have to be like a broken-field runner in a football game and change directions as often as situations evolve. I remember testifying once as an expert witness in court regarding the value of a certain horse that had died. The trial was in a small town made up of ranches, farms, and hardworking small-business owners. The attorney for the "other side" was a Chicago import who knew it all and was going to teach these country hicks a thing or two about the law. He had not deposed me (a major misjudgment on his part), so he had no idea who or what I was. Tall and leering, he actually looked like the stereotypical gangster with his black silk suit and slicked-down hair. I, on the other hand, wore a sport coat, button-down shirt, tie, and ostrich cowboy boots. His opening remark to me was "I'll try not to intimidate you." Being a well-worn, seasoned citizen, I replied, "Son, you won't intimidate me in the least."

He strutted around and tried to challenge everything I said. "Where did you get your information?" he asked. "Give me your source." Well, it just so happened I had a copy of my *Winning* series, and I held it up as I replied, "I wrote the book."

"You can't use that," he retorted. But the judge interrupted him and said, "He's quoting a source, as you asked." During recess, I knew we were on the winning side when a juror made a passing comment: "Nice boots!"

We won the case big-time, and after the trial, I walked past the attorney and said, "See, you never intimidated me a bit. Maybe you should have read the book."

There are many people you meet whom you trust right away. Others make you leery from the start. Snap judgments oftentimes prove not to be the most accurate, so I tend to trust my instincts. I was taught by my father and grandfather to look 'em in the eye, both horses and men. If they look you straight in the eye, you can probably go with your instinct. People used to ask me a lot when I was judging, "How do you pick a winner when there are so many out there to choose from?" I always replied, "It's easy if you look 'em in the eye—they'll tell you whether they're a champion or not." I find it much the same with people. Oh, I've been fooled a few times, but, looking back, really not too often.

Attitude is one of those traits or characteristics that is usually evident. The problem becomes separating it out. Sometimes it's easy to mistake cockiness for confidence or shyness for timidity, but usually if you continually look them in the eye, their true nature will surface. By the same token, so will yours.

It's interesting to notice how people become so confined in their own environment that life slips right past them. Reminds me of a couple of tales from my days when most of my training business centered around Hollywood stars. It's funny how the public views them (stars) and how they view themselves. I had horses for many celebrities; some were like everyday folks, while others seemed to be always "on stage."

Robert Taylor, who played the title role in *Billy the Kid* and hosted *Death Valley Days*, was like a father figure to me. When he was married to Barbara Stanwyck, I was a teenager galloping horses at the Marwyck Ranch during the summer months. At that time, Bob had several show horses in training with M. R. Valdez, and I had visions of becoming a race rider. After my stint in the navy, having outgrown my ability to be a jockey, I settled down in the arena. When Val retired, Bob brought his horses to me. Because of our long friendship, he wanted to help me get a leg up in the horse training business.

Private sales—to people who would hopefully keep the horse in training with me—were a big part of making a living showing horses. In those days we didn't talk about marketing or networking, just buying and selling and how to do both with the greatest return. This is where Bob came in handy. At that time, Barbara Stanwyck and Groucho Marx had long since sold Marwyck (which became Northridge Farms, a famous racing stable). Barbara and Bob had divorced, and Bob was remarried to Ursula Theiss, living not far from me in Mandeville Canyon, about a fifteen-minute drive.

Bob and I had put together a surefire plan, which worked like magic. If I had a potential client interested in buying a horse but I couldn't quite close the deal, I'd pick a time toward the end of the day for them to come one more time to "try the horse." Bob and I had a prearranged signal whereby he would call at a specified time and inquire how the transaction was coming along. If I needed help, I, in turn, would ask my customers if they were in a hurry.

It went something like this: I would tell Bob to hold the line and then would say to my customer, "One of my clients, Mr. Robert Taylor—you know, the movie actor—is on the line, and we need to talk a little business. Do you mind?" Usually, the reply was "Don't hurry, take your time." Bob and I would chat about this and that, and at the appropriate time, I would put my hand over the phone and ask my buyers if they would like to accompany my wife and me to Mr. Taylor's house for dinner. I would say that my conversation with Bob was going to take longer than expected, and we could talk about our deal on the way over and back.

No one ever turned down an invitation to dine at Robert Taylor's house, especially when Ursula fixed her famous stuffed grape leaves. Of course, as we drove over, the conversation usually centered on my friendship with Bob, the other movie-star horses in my barn, and my buyer's concern over being properly dressed. Most were nervous and excited, growing more so the closer we got to Bob's house.

Bob was always the perfect host, welcoming my clients to his home and introducing his beautiful wife Ursula. Bob said all the right things: "Oh yes, I know the horse you're interested in. Great horse; great place to ride and show out of; oh yes, I spend quite a bit of time there. I have four at the moment; yes, Don found every one for me—wouldn't go anywhere else." He was charming, and the dinner was always delightful.

After dinner, we'd excuse ourselves to finish our business and let Ursula have the floor. Once alone, Bob would anxiously ask, "How're we doing? Think we got a sale, partner?" I'd assure him the sale was forthcoming and then adjourn for the evening. With my charges safely in tow, we'd head back to my place to close the deal. Naturally, the conversation always centered on how fantastic Mr. Taylor was; a regular guy, not affected by his star status (one of the qualities that made him special). And yes, I sold the horse.

One time, though, we almost had to call the paramedics because a lady became so excited when Bob opened the door and reached for her hand that she fainted. After she revived, she was unable to speak. She just gasped and broke out in a cold sweat every time Bob got near her. We ended up having to leave without dinner, conversation, or selling a horse. Another, greeted with an extended hand, simply brushed it aside and planted a big kiss right on the lips of the very stunned movie star. Some started chattering incessantly, gushing out every word. The men would in turn stare at the gorgeous actress serving them food and drink. Bob thought maybe we should have a signal or something to prepare him for the unexpected, but it's hard to predict how people will react when confronted with a celebrity.

Bob and Ursula would take it all in stride; after all, they were helping a young horse trainer sell a horse. We even joked about how we rarely failed in our partnership (which I attribute to Bob's tutelage about business). He advised me to be honest and above board with all clients. I even made a deal with him that there was to be a money-back guarantee or free-for-another on any horse deal in which he took part. It taught me a great lesson, and I never needed to give a refund or replace any horse with which we dealt. Thinking back, we had some fun times and wild experiences as a couple of greenhorn horse traders.

But another famous personality was quite different. One day when I was at the barn, I answered the phone only to hear an unmistakable voice on the other end. "This is Be-te Da-vis. Is Mr. Burt in?" I replied that I was and asked what I could do for her. "Are you the instruc-tor who teach-es chil-dren to ride?" I assured her I was. "Well, my daugh-ter, B.D., will be there at 3:00 PM for a les-son."

The demanding, no-question tone came from a lady who was used to having her own way and giving orders, not taking them. I was quiet for a moment, somewhat taken aback. Thinking quickly, I said, "She may come at 5:00 PM for an evaluation if you like. I need to assess her aptitude for riding, as I don't want to waste anyone's time."

"My daugh-ter has talent, I can vouch for that. She will be there at three."

"Miss Davis," I said, "I think I am the one who should make that decision. Have her here at five." There was a pause on the other end, then a query: "One more thing, Mr. Burt. What do you charge for a les-son?" I quoted my price, and she candidly remarked, "Why are you twice as high as everyone else?" I answered her quite flippantly, "Because I'm twice as good." I was certain I didn't want B.D. as a client and, with that tone, was certain I would never hear from her again.

Three o'clock came and went. I got busy with other chores and headed for the house. As the clock struck five, I was at the kitchen sink looking out the window when a long, long black limousine pulled slowly into my driveway. A uniformed driver got out from behind the tinted windows and headed for the stall area. I came out of the house thinking maybe he was lost and asked if I could help.

"Are you Mr. Burt?" he asked. I decided that I was and said, "Yes."

"Mr. Burt, I have brought B.D. here for her evaluation." I almost choked but instead said, "I'll get a horse ready." He returned to the car, opened the rear door, and a lovely ten-year-old stepped out, wearing a riding habit straight out of *National Velvet*.

I visited with her for a few minutes. Yes, she had been on a pony at her sixth birthday party, she remembered, and she was led around on a horse once when her mother was on location. Why did she want to ride? "Oh," she said, "my mother said everyone is doing it, so I must."

I took her to the farthest arena, and we spent a most delightful hour together. It was the start of what would become many hours of riding, talking, and having fun over the next five or six years. We returned to the car, the door opened, and that articulate voice commanded, "Get in, young man. Sit here!" I did as I was told. We worked out the financial arrangements and, much to my surprise, became good friends. But in all the years and the many times we talked on the phone, the conversations were always preempted by "This is Be-te Da-vis." She was a very focused lady.

Attitudes, good and bad, are usually formed at an early age. Some people outgrow them but many carry that trait or attitude for life. Colts have the same tendencies. When you start to handle or halter break one, temperament is usually identified. "Oh, my colt is so smart," people say when the horse learns easily, while other horses appear stubborn or stupid given the same exercise. Be careful not to judge too quickly, because horses and people do change, and often situations dictate that adjustment. As people and horses mature, events in their lives may bring about change. Courage is often discovered during interesting times, frequently in a crisis. War and accidents are the most likely triggers that bring this attribute to the surface, which can have a lasting effect on one's future. I've known horsemen who can get bucked off and get right back on and others who got hung up and scared who never recovered their confidence. With time, some folks become more cynical, as they grow older and reflect on what might have been. Others become content with who they are and develop an attitude of self-confidence, which was there all along.

Challenges and their outcomes can have an effect on attitude. I was about twelve or thirteen, and our next-door neighbor, who was in his fifties, had worked for the same company for many years, driving some sort of tractor-type machine. One day the company was sold and new management took over. They decided to "modernize" and ordered all new types of automated equipment. He was let go because they no longer needed his expertise. He tried in vain to find another job but was told his knowledge and skills were obsolete; he had not kept up with the new technology. I watched the family fall apart. He started to drink, and his attitude became worse and worse, until he had no self-esteem left. Finally, I guess things got so unbearable that he hung himself. I vowed on that very day that no person or company would control my destiny to that extent, and to this day I have always been self-reliant. My attitude about life changed in an instant, and I became more positive, tried to stay current and to be my own person, and relied on an "I know I can" philosophy.

Roadblocks and Defeats

Early in my career, when I was a rider, an athlete, I never had any idea that it might change. Then one day that fateful riding accident became a pivotal point in my life. The doctor's prognosis: I would be in a cast for a year and probably never ride enough to make a living again. Of course I was devastated and thought, "What do I do now?" With a family to feed and no income, I was at a loss, until some of my friends suggested that since I couldn't ride, why not judge? As the saying goes, when one door closes, another one opens—and a new career was born.

I have a friend who was a superior rider with a promising career as a trainer. He went to his first show as a professional, and set the world on fire—new, creative, motivated, fresh, a star. On the way home, I'm sure still basking in his glory, he became exhausted and pulled off to the side of the road to nap. His car was struck by a truck, which left him paralyzed from the neck down. After several years in rehab, he made no progress, but his desire to train horses and students was uppermost in his mind. He never gave up that dream, and with dedication and help from others, he found a way to communicate with horses and people to produce winner after winner, year after year. He even obtained his judge's card and succeeded at that. He retired after a career spanning more than twenty-five years, and Tim Whitney was inducted into the Pacific Coast Quarter Horse Association (PCQHA) Hall of Fame.

I look at roadblocks as simply detours or times to pause and reevaluate. A change of direction may be needed, or it may mean it's time to just stop and take a breather while you ponder the situation. A roadblock doesn't have to mean the end or total defeat. Most of the time, we actually learn from our defeats, if considered with a positive approach. As each of us climbs the mountain to the next plateau, we are bound to fall down—sometimes often. It's getting up that makes the difference. My own career has had many detours, most all for the good, even though it didn't seem like it at the time.

When any door closes, we need to be prepared to walk through the one that opens. We bring some defeats on by ourselves, and it's up to us to not take that route again. I had hauled one horse for 200 miles to a show because I was leading the Pacific Coast for the year-end championship. All I needed was two points to cinch the title. It was a halter class with several entries I had beaten often before, so I didn't have any worries. I was in the holding area waiting for the class when a group of people stopped to admire my horse. We became heavily engaged in conversation, and I finally said, "Can't miss the class." Well, I got to the gate and found the class had already entered. I tried to talk the back-gate man into letting me in. "No way," he said. "The rules say once the class is called and the gate is closed, no one can enter." He was right, of course, and I had to go home and face the owners. I lost the championship by one point, which was a mistake of my own making, and I have never been late for a class or an appointment of any kind since then.

Although defeats come in many degrees, life-changing ones are always the hardest to accept or explain. They take longer to adjust to, but with persistence and a strong faith, they can prove to be a useful detour that leads us back to the path of success. Road-blocks are not nearly as devastating, I've found, and are much easier to handle. I take them as a sort of wake-up call—take a second look, change a procedure, or take a different road.

One time on my way from a convention to a meeting in New York City, I found myself in a situation where I thought I knew the rules. My interpretation, however, was slightly different than those pitching the commercial on television. I caught the red-eye express and arrived in the Big Apple at 4 AM. A tired, disheveled cowboy disembarked. While looking over the wagon train of cabs, I heard a voice over my shoulder asking if I wanted a ride to Manhattan in "a very special car, no waiting." A scab, I thought to myself. Sure, why not save a half hour or so by not waiting in line? I climbed into the limo, and the driver proceeded with idle conversation. I relaxed, and the brainpower I needed for survival was nil. Finally reaching the hotel, I stepped out into muted light and asked, "How much?" As I pulled out my wallet, the driver suddenly tripped on the curb, knocking me down and spilling the contents of my briefcase onto 54th Street. My money and hat were retrieved, but in the melee, the cabby got $125 and I got $25—the old double shuffle—not to be discovered until his taillights rounded the corner, blinking "Good-bye, sucker."

Frustrated and feeling rather stupid, I checked into my room and tried to rest awhile. I remembered I had a credit card of a special color, guaranteed to be able to buy the hotel (if I paid it off in thirty days), which I could present anywhere and immediately be handed $100, or so I thought when I listened to the commercial.

I asked the desk clerk where I could obtain a credit card cash advance, and he informed me of a bank on the next street. I phoned and begged off my meeting until later and found the bank. After a twenty-minute wait in line, the teller looked at me in disbelief when I stuck out my card and asked for $100. She told me I had to go to an office of the card endorser and not just "to any bank." In my best "Golly, gee" cowboy voice, I said, "Where might I find one of those offices, Ma'am?"

"How should I know?" she fired back at me, unimpressed by my hat or Gary Cooper twang.

I prevailed upon one of New York's finest (in blue) to point me in the direction of the closest office and again stood in line. My feeling of being able to survive in any jungle was short-lived after the teller shook his head and said, "That's not the way it's done." In answer to my quizzical look, he added, "I know they say something like that on TV, but you don't just hand us your card and we give you the money. We'll cash a check in that amount for you and use your card as ID." Now I started to panic a little. I hadn't done a banking transaction in twenty years. My wife handles that and gives me what I need. I quickly came up with, "I'm from out-of-town and don't have a check with me." He courteously replied, "No problem, we'll use a counter check. What bank?"

"What bank?" I repeated to myself, remembering our bank had recently been taken over by another. I mumbled, "I think it's the one with the stagecoaches." The clerk's head jerked up. "Oh, yes, Wells Fargo," as he looked at my non-city attire. He continued, "What branch and address?"

I said dubiously, "I think it's in the peninsula center, in Rolling Hills, California." Looking over my shoulder at the line of people, he handed me a blank check and said, "Step over there, fill this out, and come back to the front of the line."

"Thanks," was all I could muster as I backed away.

Now I'd been all grown up for years, traveled around the world, handled pressure on a daily basis. All I wanted was $100—surely I could do this. I filled out the check and returned to the window. He took the check and, looking slightly annoyed with me, started with, "You don't make it out to us," as he crossed out the first line. "It's supposed to say cash, and you put the amount in the wrong place. Now, let me compare your signature with that on your card." He turned the card over only to witness the fact I had never signed it. Pushing it towards me, I signed in the space provided. To this day I'm certain he only gave me the money to get rid of me. I was also sure that the check, in its reworked state, would never surface at my bank. But it did.

I made it to my meeting quite late and actually left town with money in my wallet, together with a lesson learned. Rules or instructions should be read for oneself and not left to the interpretation of others, who may or may not have read them. Also, I've added this little transaction to my list of don'ts, along with buses and subways, when in New York!

Youth is so eager to charge forward, and I fit right into that category when I was judging one of my first horse shows in Hawaii. I was literally in paradise and was invited back to judge almost yearly after that for a couple of decades. Following the show was the usual luau, giving me the opportunity to visit with the people. One conversation centered on the cost of bringing horses over and keeping them in the islands.

Those who really wanted to show barged their horses, trailers, trucks, and tack from island to island. They'd spend a few days and barge back. Feed, being scarce and costly, had to be brought in from the mainland (for the most part), and feed stores rationed it out to customers.

On the plane ride home, I pondered the logistics for islanders who wanted to show or just keep a horse to trail ride. The next morning, as I strolled along the beach to my favorite coffee shop, I noticed the kelp barge harvesting its crop. It's a peculiar-looking boat, sort of a floating combine hugging the shoreline scooping up kelp. I wondered what they used all that kelp for? When I got to the local hangout where coffee, conversation, and the solution to the world's problems flowed freely, I asked if anyone knew about the kelp barge.

I was informed it worked seven days a week up and down the coast harvesting kelp. In fact, there was a kelp factory in San Pedro (not far from my house) that processed it into food supplements sold at health stores, as well as "some kinda cow or goat feed supplement."

My spirits buoyed—I knew I had probably stumbled onto a great discovery. "Borderline genius," I thought to myself. What an idea, a kelp-based horse feed made into cubes or ground feed. All I needed was a formula and the necessary machinery and behold, a new industry in the islands! I hurried home, my mind racing through all the usual inspiring mottos that hang in student dorm rooms, along with my own personal saying: "Act, don't react." I got on the phone and called the plant manager, dockmaster, barge skipper, and anyone remotely connected with the harvesting and manufacturing of kelp products.

Weeks were spent gathering data. Because I bothered so many people, I'm sure my name spread rapidly throughout the kelp industry. I called my accountant and prepared an elaborate prospectus, listing all known elements of kelp as a feed supplement, the costs to start, costs to maintain, and of course the profit when I introduced this phenomenon to the islands.

During my many trips to Hawaii, dating back to when I sailed into Pearl Harbor on a navy destroyer, I met several entrepreneurs. I put in a call to Earl Thacker, the leading influence in the islands. For over an hour, I described in detail my elaborate plan to bring inexpensive horse feed to Hawaii so the industry could boom and thrive. He listened intently, not once interrupting or dampening my enthusiasm. After I exhausted all my reasons why he should participate as a savior of the equine industry, he said, "Don, that's the greatest idea I've ever heard." Upon hearing that, I almost jumped the Pacific Ocean with joy. "However," he continued, "there's one problem I don't think you've taken into consideration."

"What's that?" I questioned.

"We don't have kelp in Hawaii."

Pondering Point

PONDERING POINT

When I was confronted with some kind of an obstacle, usually I'd saddle my horse and ride to a place where I could look one way and see the vast ocean and look the other way to the mountain. My kids used to call it Dad's Pondering Point. When things got rough or I was dealt a setback, it was a place to sort out problems, reroute any detours, and count my blessings.

I've had many blessings, but I didn't think the one that stands out the most was a blessing at the time. One of the best Christmas presents I remember as a kid was my first very own saddle. A box as big as I was with my name on it stood out under the tree. I looked at that box for days hoping for it to move or magically open. On Christmas morning, even after I opened it and found my wish had come true, it was hard to believe. I even sat in my saddle on the floor while I ate breakfast.

Then my grandfather walked over and picked it up with me in tow. Outside we went, straight for the water trough. He never said a word, just threw my new blessing into the water. I started to cry. He told me to go get my horse. After he let it soak for a long time, he saddled my horse and said, "Now, ride it till it's dry." I was still sobbing, but I did as I was told. That saddle molded to my shape and was the most comfortable saddle I ever rode in. The power of my grandfather's wisdom changed one little boy's perception of blessings. Now I wear a shirt that reads OLD GUYS RULE!

When I got a call from the original owner of *Horse & Rider* magazine, Ray Rich, it turned out to be another unrecognized blessing. He wanted to interview me for a story he was doing. Afterwards he asked if I'd be interested in writing a monthly article. This was back in 1969. Having no journalism background, I thought, "How in the world can I do this?" I ran it by my father-in-law, who was an attorney, and he asked, "What are you going to write about? Won't it be hard to think up a new topic each month?" I had done some writing, mainly about Frosty, my trick horse, which was a book in the back of my mind.

But nothing ventured, nothing gained, as the old saying goes. Until the magazine was sold in 1991, I found it was not difficult to find something to write about each month. In the meantime, I had also started writing a monthly column for the *Quarter Horse Journal*, and I continue to do so today. This experience eventually led to the publishing of five books about horses— some technical, some human interest—and an agent who took me under his wing and has become a great friend. It brought about a self-published newsletter called *The Don Burt Equiletter*, an economic analysis serving the horse industry during the mid-eighties. It was a venture that needed more capital than I had at the time, but it whetted my appetite to expand my horizons during the transition from judging and teaching to the next plateau.

Another deviation along the way that turned out to be a blessing was the formation of Equestrian Consultants Inc. in 1973. I had an inquiry from the president of Transamerica Development Co., who needed some advice regarding one of his equestrian–real estate developments. I don't quite remember how he got my name, but he needed someone with expertise regarding horse shows that were being put on at the equestrian center, which was the hub of the development. They had been losing money ever since they opened, and the board of directors wanted to know why. I met with the board, who were very heavy hitters in the real estate business but knew little or nothing about horse shows and running an equestrian center. I offered my services, for a fee, and they hired me. I went home and related this new turn of events to my trusty father-in-law, who promptly decided we needed to form a corporation. He set everything up, and I instantly became president of this newly formed enterprise.

After I did a behind-the-scenes probe of the center's books and management, I was appalled. No wonder they were not making ends meet. The present manager and his cronies were cooking the books and getting kickbacks from every supplier involved in putting on the shows. After I made my report and pointed out that this kind of unscrupulous conduct was not the general rule in the horse business, it didn't take long for the board to fire the culprits. I found myself in charge of making the facility profitable, or at least able to break even. I filled the barn with horses that belonged to customers of a couple of trainers I had enticed to move in and hired a reputable show manager to put on the events. My wife managed the books, billed the customers, and paid the expenses, and I had to answer to the board once a month. Our newly formed company was thriving. Instead of managing the facility for only one year, I was there nine years, until the development company eventually turned over the equestrian center to the homeowners, as stipulated in their deeds.

During those management years, I found that there was a real need for expertise in the building and maintaining of horse facilities, and I was lucky enough to have the only company proficient in this field at that time. Over the years, it expanded and became a full-service consulting firm specializing in feasibility studies, site planning, operational requirements, and customizing the right equestrian operation for a specific area. I had people calling me from Hawaii to New Jersey and everywhere in between with projects ranging from private communities to fairgrounds and horse parks. Little did I know when I formed the corporation that it would survive for thirty-five years—and all because of my knowledge of the horse.

While I was managing the equestrian center for Transamerica, the president had a brainstorm and sought to go beyond the initial program of establishing a physical facility for horsemen and women to use. It was his desire to provide an expanded program for the horse enthusiast. His idea was to form an affiliation with a riding club in England, whereby each facility would extend reciprocal privileges to the other. This affiliation, bringing together a riding establishment from each country, was to be known as a "sistership." The Centre, which housed some of the best shows in the country and also the horses belonging to Princess Anne, was just outside of London.

This afforded my wife and I our first journey abroad. Along with the company president and his wife, we were royally received. The ceremony took place at Hickstead following the Nation's Cup, a team type of jumping competition that included teams from all over Europe plus our own U.S. team. Proceeding to the press tent, we witnessed the exchange of plaques that officially designated the "sistership." After the welcome and a series of speeches, the engraving on the plaques was read: "Whereby the members of both clubs are free and welcome to enjoy the benefits of either club. July, 1971, AD." Each owner then exchanged documents, which were put on display at both centers. I was very impressed and quite honored to be a part of this affiliation.

Role Models and Their Philosophies

I've had many role models, and I've always valued their advice and methods. Some I knew well, some not at all, but I heeded what they said. From Jimmy Williams: "It's what you learn after you know it all that counts." Also, "You can read a person by looking them in the eye. You should read your horse by observing his ears."

From Theodore Roosevelt's "The Man in the Arena" speech: "It is not the critic who counts; not the man who points out how the strong man stumbles, or where the doer of deeds could have done them better. The credit belongs to the man who is actually in the arena, whose face is marred by dust and sweat and blood; who strives valiantly; who errs, who comes short again and again, because there is no effort without error and shortcoming; but who does actually strive to do the deeds; who knows great enthusiasms, the great devotions; who spends himself in a worthy cause; who at the best knows in the end the triumph of high achievement, and who at the worst, if he fails, at least fails while daring greatly, so that his place shall never be with those cold and timid souls who neither know victory nor defeat."

I always admired the Olympic athletes, as well as the world champion cowboy Trevor Brazile and champion golfer Tiger Woods. To keep on top, they put in the work and are up before dawn to practice. Champion team roper Leo Camarillo had the ability and the same desires, along with an innovative side. Most heelers threw loops in front of the steer's back legs, a trap for the steer to step into. Leo and his brother Jerold discovered that when the steer turns, both hind feet are off the ground for a second, and they roped at that time, shaving seconds off their time.

But one role model always stands out above all the rest. My dad. I have not known a stronger person in my life—not in terms of muscle and body strength but rather his strong constitution and deep faith and the courage of his convictions. No one I have ever come across had the obstacles to overcome that he had. I never once heard him complain. He would smile, accept the challenge, and go forward. He truly believed in me when I doubted myself.

I remember in the early 1970s, I took my dad with me to Washington, D.C., where I was judging a horse show. I had brought him along to visit his oldest sister, who was getting up in years. The show was over, and Dad had had a memorable week. It was now time to get to Dulles Airport for our early-morning flight. Another horse show judge was going to give us and a few other show officials a ride. When he didn't show up on time, we went to his room and found him passed out on the bed, still in his tuxedo. We pinned a note to his chest saying we had borrowed his car and took off. None of us knew exactly how to get to the airport, just the general direction. I was driving, and Dad was sitting in the back seat, not saying a word. With seven of us crammed in the car along with our luggage and everyone talking at once, it was chaos. Even after I took the wrong road, broke all speed limits weaving in and out of traffic, and had to back down an off-ramp at one point, as scared as my dad looked, he only said, "If you'd all just be quiet, my son will get us there safely and on time." An hour and a half later, I saw the sign to the airport. We had fifteen minutes to spare, and the gas tank was on empty. We left the car with the show steward, an authoritative, no-nonsense kind of lady, who was going to drive it back to the owner. We checked our luggage. As we headed for the terminal, I turned to wave to Iris, who was arguing with a policeman about moving the car from the tow-away zone. I knew she could handle it, so we hurried to the gate, where they were holding the plane.

My dad faced life and death with the same smile of sheer determination. He was a true gentleman in every sense of the word and a leader without seeking to be one. I remember him telling me, "No matter what you do in life, give it your all. Strive to be the best, whether digging ditches or training horses, and if you're good, they'll find you."

My dad had cancer and lived with us the last several years of his life, with never a complaint, even on a bad day filled with pain. We finally had to put him in the hospital, and after only a couple of days, he took a major turn for the worse. After my morning chores, I always went to see him. He was propped up in bed, and he said to me, "Call your brother. I'll wait until he gets here." I had no idea what was happening but complied with his request and called my brother, who lived a couple of hours away. I also called my wife, who immediately came to the hospital. We talked about all sorts of things—the horses, our lives, the kids—as we waited for my brother to arrive.

When he came into the room, my dad asked him how he and his family were. During the conversation, he suddenly said, "Kiss me good-bye, boys." We were stunned but complied with his wish. We had always kissed our father hello and good-bye all of our lives, so it was not out of the ordinary. We held his hands, one son on each side. After we kissed him, he passed on with his eyes wide open. He was eager to face whatever was next with the same determination he had shown throughout his life. He had the most peaceful look on his face, so I knew his soul had ascended to heaven. When the nurse came in, she tried to close his eyes but they would not shut. We all looked at each other and realized our father had actually chosen when to leave, and he did it on his own terms. If death can be beautiful, we had just been witnesses. To this day, whenever I feel a little down or things aren't going just right, my dad always comes to mind.

Many people before and since have played important parts in my life and career, and I regard them as role models, so to speak. Everyone needs a little help along the way. But for me, a real role model is someone who has had great personal success and has earned the respect of others in business, family, or personal relationships. A role model whose philosophies are unselfish can often instill in others the confidence they may be lacking. These are mentors I look to, not so much for what they do or did but rather for who they really are inside. That makes them stand out in my mind.

Believe in Yourself

"To thine own self be true."

Wisdom is knowing what to do, knowledge is knowing how to do it, and success is doing it.

Great people never look into the mirror and think, "I'm the greatest." They ask themselves, "Am I the best I can be?"

Some may call you an overachiever, but if you truly believe in yourself, you'll never give up until you find a way.

There is no disgrace in being knocked down; the disgrace is not getting up.

My dad had a saying that he instilled in me early on. "If you coast, you soon come to a stop, unless you're going downhill." That advice has been a mainstay in my life. After watching ten rounds of the National Finals Rodeo recently, it came to mind. Those guys and gals don't coast or quit; they cowboy up with each performance despite a bad draw, hurting neck, sore back, or torn ligament. They belly up to the task. I conjured up aches and pains just watching the rough stock riders get slammed into the ground night after night. The contests were so close, the top scores yo-yoed with every performance. Even when I thought that a ride couldn't be topped, the next one made a liar out of me. Of course, that's why they're the best in the world.

After horse shows and rodeos, San Francisco's Cow Palace was the big attraction during my early twenties. I was showing good horses, winning a lot, and thought I could do no wrong. The world was my oyster. My dad would come with me, driving one of the vans. He'd help get me ready. He had rodeoed a lot and knew many of the cowboys who hung around the chutes. After every performance, the horse trainers and rodeo contestants headed for The Chinaman or Dirty Eddie's, a saloon on the waterfront. More horses were "ridden" in the saloon under the influence of "courage boosters" than ever were under saddle in the Cow Palace, which is something that doesn't happen much today.

I had a winning week and was getting to think my luck couldn't last until the championships. But when that weekend rolled around, my horses seemed to just get better, and I actually won several championships in multi-disciplines. However, when it came time for the last jumper championship, I was a little tired and so was the horse. I'd already won more than my share and was assured of eating throughout the winter. So I told the owners not to bother to come to the show that evening because I was just going to jump a couple of fences and pull the horse up.

My dad had listened to what I'd said and was silent as he and I started getting the horse ready. I walked the course in a haphazard sort of way and warmed up a little over a couple of fences in the alleyway, my dad watching. I had drawn the last slot, so I had time to monitor several horses. I was just about to mount up when my dad said, "Son, I'm a little disappointed in you." My dad rarely gave me unsolicited advice, and I asked him why. He said, "You've already won a lot of classes, more than ever before, so now you're going to up and quit without even trying. I didn't raise you to be a ..." He just walked away and never finished the sentence.

When I arrived at the gate, I realized no horse and rider pair had gone clean. The leading horse had a half fault (a hind rub). My plan was still to pull up after a couple of fences; it was late and time to go home. I jumped the first obstacle, the second, and the third of twelve. The horse was jumping well. By now, I found myself halfway around the course with no faults. I jumped a couple more fences cleanly. Then my mind finally came out of remission and I told myself, "If you coast now, you may start the downhill slide or stop going forward and get too comfortable".

The last jump was at the far end of the arena—it was time to make the decision. I was scared to death; maybe I'd make a mistake and blow it. As we approached, I checked, spurred, took back, and moved forward, clearing the fence with inches to spare. Another win under our belt. My dad never said a word, but the smile on his face gave me a clue.

We celebrated that night with cowboys and jump jockeys, all telling stories. The owners stopped by and said they had watched the class. They knew once I got into the pen, I couldn't quit or let up even a little. That was one of the biggest lessons of my life.

My dad had a lot of sayings and was always the optimist. There were times when we had next to nothing, and he would joke and say, "If we had some ham, we'd have some ham and eggs, if we had some eggs." Then we'd make do with what we had. This was particularly true during his rodeoing era, when the pickins were slim.

I think sayings can have a great influence on your life. Here's a little psychology from an old cowboy: "Never let a horse or rider know what they can't do." Here are some from my dad, who spoke little but said volumes.

- "If you think you're beaten, you are."
- "If you think you dare not, you don't."
- "If you'd like to win but think you can't, it's almost a cinch you won't."
- "If you think you'll lose, you've already lost."

For in this world you'll find it's all in your state of mind.

Motivational speeches have been used for years; pep talks are standard in any locker room before the game. If your body is in great condition, and you're ready for the challenge, make sure your mind focuses on victory.

In a group, if the deck is stacked against you or you don't have the votes, those who believe in themselves don't hesitate to swim upstream and buck the odds. They not only try but convince others to follow their approach. Oh, there are the snake-oil salesmen and slick politicians who can sway most folks with words that might convince those who are just followers. But true leaders are self-assured and not afraid to think for themselves. They act on the belief that often comes from doing their homework, whether physical or mental, which usually makes the believer the most prepared.

There is a flip side to this—understanding your limitations. I would have loved to have become a jockey, but my size changed that desire. I could do nearly the same thing by riding jumping horses or working cattle, which gave me the same satisfaction. When I couldn't ride anymore, judging filled the bill. This allowed me to carry out the courage of my convictions, especially when other judges time after time had placed a certain horse first and I liked him third. Believe in yourself enough to stand alone and do what you believe, instead of following the others.

This reminds me of what happened once when I was judging an all-breed show. The Tennessee Walking Horse judge mysteriously disappeared before the last class he was to adjudicate. They asked me if I would fill in. "Sure," I said. "Why not?" I quickly read the rules governing the class and proceeded to have the ringmaster call the gaits. I kind of had in mind which horses the other judge had placed all day long and knew the ones they applauded and those they booed when the horses didn't please the crowd. There was an added stipulation to the rules for this particular class, a "pleasure class," that clearly stated, but most often ignored, no bar shoes. As the horses performed, I noticed all had bar shoes. After I lined them up for inspection, I called the show steward into the arena. He is the official that interprets the rules and makes sure the judge and exhibitors follow them. As I went down the line, I had my ringmaster pick up a front foot of every horse and, with a big to-do, I crossed off the number on my card. After I finished eliminating all of the horses, I went to the microphone and announced, "In my opinion, all of the horses in the class violated the rules and are hereby eliminated. As no one qualified for a prize, this has been a fine demonstration. If all the entries will leave the arena, we'll go on with the horse show." Well, the riders were livid, as no judge had ever complied completely with the rule; it evidently was a rule that had been disregarded for some time. On my way out of the arena, one rider rode over to me (it was a horse that had been winning all day) and said to me in a loud voice, "You dirty old man!" I knew then that the other judge had been intimidated so badly all day that he wanted no part of this class.

Later, I received a letter from the organization thanking me for having the courage to follow the rules. I knew I was right and believed in myself enough to not be swayed. As I told one exhibitor later, if you don't like the rule, change it, but don't ignore it. After this show, I got very active in the rule-making process, because if there are rules that I must play by, I want to help make them.

EXCELLENCE

Excellence can be attained if you care more than others think is wise, dream more than others think is practical, and expect more than others think is possible.

Follow Your Dream

"Climb every mountain, ford every stream, follow every rainbow till you find your dream." Those are words in a song, but early in life I heard another song: "Gonna Build Me a Mountain." And that I set out to do. I've changed directions several times but always followed my heart and never lost sight of my dream. I set many goals for myself and believed that a goal is like a dream with a deadline. I've done a great deal of reading and decided that life is a story. How you tell it is what counts. I never lost sight of what I truly wanted. To me, success is achieving your goals while doing unto others as you would like them to do unto you. Climb the mountain from plateau to plateau, staying on one long enough to prepare for the next. I truly believe if you take your dream up the mountain, happiness will be there.

I've always said I have an angel on each shoulder. When it was obvious to everyone but me that my training career was over after the accident that put me in a cast for a year, my friends started hiring me to judge. The arena opened its gates again, and a whole new career was born. It allowed me to put my background of observation and participation into play. I could be creative and decisions came easy; no pressure did I ever feel. But that was not the end. My dream was to be the best horseman of my day—not rider or trainer but horseman. Judging opened the door to teaching, and clinics and lecturing were right up my alley, me being a bit of a ham and all.

Many associations hired me to teach their judges' seminars, which qualified the attendees to maintain their judge's card (license) for a period of time. The American Quarter Horse Association (AQHA) sent me all around the world to preside over their seminars and to qualify international judges. I also did a lot of public speaking (told horse stories) and lectured at colleges and universities that had equestrian programs. It seemed there was no end to the avenues that opened up for me.

Because I seemed to be everywhere, doing everything, I was asked to serve on boards and committees. I enjoyed the challenge of leadership and became the first professional horseman to serve as president of the AQHA, the world's largest breed association. I didn't realize it at the time, but my mother's earlier words came to fruition after all. My wanting to be a horse trainer led to eventually becoming president, which fulfilled not only my dream but hers also. I was asked to write and put my knowledge and thoughts on paper, which came easily. I've said many times that even though I've put in a lot of hours, I don't feel like I've worked a day in my life; I just played horseman, truly a dream come true.

People have often asked me what it was like being president of the AQHA, and I sum it up like this: It was kind of like trying to saddle a horse in the midst of a whirlwind … a bit overwhelming, to say the least. The momentum takes hold the very first meeting when you're asked to join ranks with the other four members at the head table. From that moment on, for the next five years, your life is not the same. You become an ambassador, a spokesperson for the association, overseeing a membership of over 350,000. Each year a new member comes on board, and you move up the ladder until you finally become president.

After being voted in at that first directors' luncheon, my phone never stopped ringing. My fax machine died several times from pure exhaustion, and my mailman had to beef up the suspension on his truck to carry the load. I'm not sure anything can prepare a person for the experience. Even in the aftermath, it was hard to get back to normal. I almost wanted to stop the world, so I could get off. My tenure, however, wasn't all work. I assure you the laughs were many and the people I met along the way became the greatest gratification of all.

The years flew by, and I chalked up one experience after the other. Many trails were ridden, as the AQHA increased its exposure internationally. My last year was especially rewarding, as it allowed me to travel and spread the Quarter Horse gospel. The cattle drive and branding I was privileged to attend, along with the chuck-wagon nights, the campfires, and songs, fulfilled my lifelong dream. I guess camaraderie would best describe it.

We made quite a splash targeting a worldwide audience at the Atlanta Olympic Games and again at the National Horse Show at Madison Square Garden for the debut of the Cowboy Hat. While at the Olympics, the AQHA put on all the demonstrations during the halftime breaks in preparation for reining someday becoming the first Western-discipline Olympic event. Accepted by the United States Equestrian Team as a discipline, reining is now a competition in the World Equestrian Games (WEG), just a stepping-stone away from international acceptance in the Olympic Games … a dream that hopefully will become a reality in my lifetime.

Along with Olympic riders from all over the world, I watched the first reining rider enter the arena at the WEG in Jerez, Spain, in 2002. A brand-new arena had been built for the games that year, and a "dirt specialist" was brought in from the United States. It was not an easy task to convince people (through a translator) that didn't understand what was so *importante* about dirt. Weeks before, the specialist had gone ground-searching in the areas around the town. In the side of a hill, he found his "red dirt" and had it hauled to the site. When the first Western rider ever to compete in the WEG made her first stop, Dr. Dirt breathed a sigh of relief—the ground was perfect.

Several of us were invited to sit in the royal box, where Queen Sofia of Spain and the Infanta, Doña Pilar de Borbón (sister of the king), were clapping along with each run. A member of our Quarter Horse contingency was explaining to the queen the different maneuvers and how they were scored. We had a storybook finish: the U.S.A cinched team gold, Canada took the silver, and Italy the bronze. The United States won both the individual gold and silver, and Canada garnered the bronze.

One of the most touching moments happened at the victory party. A young Spanish boy came every day to watch the practice sessions. He took a special liking to

Shawn Flarida, the individual gold winner, and dogged after him daily. One day he asked Shawn for his hat; he wanted to be a cowboy like his hero. Each day he would ask, until finally Shawn told the boy if he won the gold medal he would indeed give the boy his hat. With two gold medals hanging from his neck, Shawn headed to the press conference and the barn. There was the boy, waiting. As he had promised, Shawn took off his hat and put it on the boy's head. I've never seen a happier scene—the boy almost cried with happiness. However, he quickly begged off because he was already late for work.

During the reception party in the tent the U.S. team shared with Great Britain, Shawn motioned for me to come with him. We went back through the kitchen to the last basin, where I saw the Spanish boy, hat worn proudly, washing dishes. As we walked back through the crowd, I was now even prouder of my cowboy hat and being an American.

I've come a long way up the mountain from the river bottom in Burbank and am forever grateful for all the help and experiences that have made my journey so fruitful. My path has taken me on several trips to Israel, where I judged and gave clinics. Under high security, led by VIP tour guides, my wife and I were fortunate to be able to spend a night on a kibbutz (a cooperative) that had a horse program. We attended the races in Nazareth, stood at the edge of the Sea of Galilee where Jesus fed the masses, floated in the Dead Sea, climbed the Masada (a massive stone plateau that once was King Herod's palace), prayed at the Western Wall in Jerusalem, visited the birthplace of Christ in Bethlehem, and had dinner with a Bedouin sheik under a tent in the middle of the desert, surrounded by loose camels. One final stop took us to a riding stable, patterned after a guest ranch, that boasted Western riding and five-day treks for sleeping under the stars ... a cross between cowboy and Bedouin. As we left, we captured on film their slogan stamped on a bumper sticker: Shalom Y'all.

I also care very much for others whose dreams have come true. I have followed the career of Professional Rodeo Cowboys Association (PRCA) tie-down roper Stran Smith, partly because he is married to Jennifer, a former Miss Rodeo America queen who is like a member of our family. She and Stran went together off and on while both pursued careers of their own. He is a top rodeo performer and she a TV newswoman and color commentator at rodeos, races, and other horse-sports activities. They finally tied the knot, and she settled in to raising a family, while Stran kept trying to win the "gold buckle" year after year, contending for the elusive title of world champion. He came very close to winning on many occasions over the nine or ten years that I know of, but it was always just out of sight. First a heart procedure, then a shoulder operation, hindered competition. It seemed like every time he caught a glimpse of success, fate would take him down. Never a quitter, he'd "cowboy up" and face all challenges. Time was running short for him, hampered by setbacks and trying to vie with other athletes much younger than him. Seems like he always had an uphill pull. Again he was going strong when a freak accident killed his best horse, and without a top mount he once more nearly gave up. But no—"try" was his favorite word, as halfway through the season he went searching for a horse to carry him to the National Finals Rodeo (NFR) finals. It seemed like an impossible task, but he was lucky and came across one that had been retired and turned out. He and the horse clicked right away, and it wasn't long before he was a contender again. But how do you make up all that lost ground? He was kind of like a racehorse finding himself behind the pack on the homestretch. I think nearly everyone who knew Stran was cheering him on in his quest to challenge the leaders.

Night after night, he performed well but not on top. Inching his way along, it came down to the last performance. He was ahead in the averages, which meant a big payday, but he had to rope his last calf in under eight seconds to keep any lead. Hollywood writers could not have written a more fitting climax. He roped and tied his calf in 7.5 seconds, and the world championship was finally his. It just so happened his wife, Jennifer, was doing the TV color commentary that night and had to interview all the winners. She couldn't contain herself; when he came up to the mike, she ran to meet him and jumped into his arms, and their hugs and kisses were witnessed by millions on TV. When asked how he felt, his statement was, "Never give up on your dream." His gold buckle was a symbol for all, and the saying proved true. As a side note, the horse he finally found ironically enough was named Destiny, long before Stran came along.

There is a poem in the movie 8 *Seconds*, which is the life story of Lane Frost, bull rider, who was killed in the arena at an early age. However, he became a world champion before his death and was the youngest cowboy ever inducted into the PRCA Hall of Fame. I only remember the last couple of lines from the poem: "The bandage and pain, rodeo was his legacy and cowboy was his name." His dream from when he could first talk was to be a world champion bull rider, which he accomplished.

Reminds me of another saying about following your dream: "There are many exits on the freeway to success. If by chance you take a wrong one, you can always find the next on-ramp and get back on track."

Every now and again, if I kind of slacked off on preparation, my dad used to say, "Son, you're getting a little too big for your britches." It took years for this to sink in. Even when I was a member of the AQHA Executive Committee, I discovered I needed to refresh my memory. The reminder appeared on one of our monthly "things to do" agendas. Who was going to represent the AQHA in the sponsors' cutting at the National Cutting Horse Association's summer spectacular classic? All of the associate members were either away or had pressing business. Guess who that left? I really wanted to do it anyway, or at least it sounded great at the time. All my old armchair-athlete cronies were green-eyed when I told them I was showing a cutting horse in Fort Worth.

A few months prior, the NCHA office wrote asking me for a bio, picture, and hat size—star-status goodies. If I had thought about it then, I'd have realized my britches were getting mighty snug. But I thought, "This will be a piece of cake". Four or five "wannabes" would be strutting our stuff on Saturday night in front of the real cutters.

I was informed there would be a riders' clinic before the show. Great, a chance to polish my skills. Fully intending to ride my horse every day at home, practice was actually put off until a week before the event. I managed to squeeze in two days of spinning, sliding, and galloping, hoping to shape up in two half-hour sessions. What's to worry? I was born in the saddle and can ride anything ...

My mind being that of a twenty-five-year-old, I forgot the seat of my pants was forty years older. I should have read the signs or omens. Two days before my wife and I were to depart, our airline tickets had not arrived. Our trusty travel agent assured me they had been sent two days earlier via FedEx. I still panicked, until they finally arrived a few hours before departure.

Arriving at Dallas-Fort Worth Airport, we were whisked to our hotel and then to the riders' dinner. My spirits dampened slightly when I found out there were sixteen riders, some of whom showed all the time and had brought their own horses, saddles, and trainers. I had my Sparks Rust spurs and well-worn chaps, which had been let out in every seam. I had no idea who my trainer was nor what horse I was to ride until someone at our table said, "Oh, you've got one of the best trainers, and he'll probably have you ride Widow-Maker." At the time the name meant nothing to me.

After margaritas and enchiladas, all the riders were to pick one of the piñatas that decorated the room. When all sixteen piñatas had been chosen, the MC told us to turn each one over to find a number tucked on the underside. This was to detemine our work order. I drew number 13. Some chuckled, some gave condolences. My wife congratulated me and said, "It's your lucky number. At least you don't have to go first."

We were to practice at three the next afternoon and show at seven that evening. In the morning, we headed for the arena to find my appointed trainer and check out my horse. We got to the practice pen and quickly recognized my teacher from a picture on a bulletin board we had seen en route. I introduced myself. After we talked, I had another panic attack. He had thought the special sponsor cutting was the next day. My horse was still at the ranch, two hours away. "No problem," he said and hurried to find someone to bring my mount there by 3:00 PM. It was now noon.

We returned for my lesson at 2:30 and found my pro schooling a big-moving, quick athlete of a horse. It was lesson time, and I was first gunner. No warm-up, no lope, no trot, no nothing! I was to go into the herd and cut out a cow with 200 eyes watching me. I thought they'd at least let me ride around and get accustomed to the horse. What happened to the clinic? While this great horse ducked and dived, I not only perspired, I changed my lavender shirt to dark purple in a matter of seconds just trying to stay on his back. I was over-mounted, to say the least, and when my five-minute session finished, never in my life had I felt so inadequate.

I went back to the hotel to rest and gather my thoughts, wondering what in the world I had gotten myself into. My wife, white as a sheet, assured me I didn't look that bad. I knew otherwise.

Seven o'clock came, and the first twelve cutters were scoring 210, 220, 223, and so forth. No one fell off yet; they were all good. I finally got to warm up, and my consummate-professional trainer coached me every step of the way, cramming more cutting expertise into my head than I'll ever use in my lifetime. I slowly began to feel a diluted amount of confidence return to the pit of my stomach.

I was next. I raised my hand, passed the start marker, pulled my hat down, and prayed. When I exited, everyone said I looked great, a real pro, and congratulated me. I scored a 222, one point out of first place. You know, reserve champion isn't half bad for a Don Quixote–type impossible dreamer like me.

Family and Friends

I have been blessed. I not only have an angel on each shoulder but a father who instilled in me strength of purpose and a work ethic that never quits. Whatever you set out to do, be the best. Whether a bricklayer or brain surgeon, it makes no difference. You can do and be anything you want if you want it badly enough. Family and friends are closely related to your success. My family always supported everything I tried, and horse-business friends are like family. There's a kinship and closeness not found in many other businesses. As I grew older, I realized just how important family and friends are, and I cherish them more each day. It is truly an honor to be referred to as a horseman.

I remember many moons ago when the warm-up arena announcer drowned out " . . . the land of the free and the home of the brave" with "Get an ambulance, we need a doctor now!" The class had been called to the back gate, and the first entry was ready to go when longtime stock horse trainer Ora Rhodes collapsed on his horse and fell to the ground. Heart attack was the diagnosis, and all moved aside for the paramedics. Ora had two horses entered in the stock horse stake. His number was being called, and Clyde Kennedy and Mac McHugh bailed off their own mounts, each mounting one of Ora's. Without hesitation, they showed the horses to their best ability. Both Clyde and Mac had competing entries in the class, but camaraderie and a sense of family overshadowed their own competitive spirit. As it turned out, Ora survived; Clyde was first, and Mac was second with Ora's two horses. Beating their own horses and handing the championship to Ora Rhodes went much deeper than sportsmanship.

I'm a firm believer in networking. Even when you're not actively seeking help, that's when family and friends step up to the plate. Almost without a plan, when one member is in need, the network goes to work, and people we may not even know usually come forward. It is never more evident than during disasters, either national, local, or personal; people appear almost out of nowhere to help. Blood donors don't wait for a crisis to occur, they pitch in before the fact. But closer to home, most of the time you don't have to ask. The feeling of someone being in your corner is comforting.

I have had several personal experiences when it has happened to me. When I was just starting out on my own, broke but full of vim and vigor, I happened to have won the two classes leading up to the championship class. At that time I didn't own a hunt coat but was instead showing in just an ordinary sport jacket. This was a jumper stake, and one friend, who rode for a private stable and had a whole wardrobe, suddenly appeared with a hunt coat. "Here, wear this," he said. "It has always brought me luck." I won the class. Afterwards, when I tried to return the coat, he said, "Looks like it's your lucky coat too. Keep it, it's yours." I went on to win many championships, several wearing that coat. As I was looking through an old tack trunk I had long since put away, I came across that coat, folded and with my number still pinned on the back. It was the coat I wore when I won my very last class as a jumping-horse rider. It had indeed brought me luck, not only in the show ring but through the spirit of friendship and shared memories.

Another time early in my career, I was hauling six horses from a show in Indio, California, to one held in Phoenix, Arizona. Halfway there I blew the engine and had to be towed to a garage. There I was, in the middle of nowhere, stranded with six horses 150 miles from the show. I still don't know how word travels so fast in the horse business (no cell phones in those days), but before long a van pulled up along with two pickups and trailers ready to load up all the tack, clothes, and horses to get me to the show on time.

Nowhere is friendship more evident than every weekend at the rodeo. Those who compete against each other are often traveling partners, sharing expenses and anything else to help out a friend. They are in the chutes pulling their bull rope or adjusting a saddle, critiquing their own buck-off so it won't happen to a friend. They are the first to cheer when a buddy makes a good ride or has a good time in those events. Even if it beats their score, genuine joy bursts forth.

Of course, family is the backbone of any champion. Having someone in your corner instills confidence and the desire to do well. Family members bring a lot of security to our daily lives. Whether in a horse show or rodeo, racing or riding for pleasure, we always need a ground person, someone who is honest with their evaluation. They bring you back to reality, like when my dad used to say, "I think you're getting a little too big for your britches, son."

When I watch championship golf, I'm amazed at how often the leader confers with his caddy on how to play the hole. In football, baseball, basketball, or any professional sport, there seems to be a coach for every element, starting with Little League and soccer. Many times the coach is as close as Mom, who is usually the driver but has an opinion too. In fact, I can't think of a successful individual, whether in business or sports, that doesn't have someone they can bounce things off of and get an honest opinion. Nothing pumps someone up like encouragement or someone who believes in you, win, lose, or draw. They are the people I refer to as friends.

We all have many acquaintances who we think of as friends, but as the years go by and our lives take on a different look or direction, we can look back on the people who are still there, through thick and thin. Whether related to you or not, they have never wavered on your behalf, even when you've been dead wrong. These are the folks that I refer to as friends. They expect nothing in return, but every time you fall, theirs is the first hand you see when you need help to get up. I've come across horses in my career who I could count on to give their best, and they too I call friends. Even though we don't choose our families, we do choose our friends. I find in the end they are there for you during and after your ascent up the mountain.

A year or so ago, my wife and I attended a convention in San Francisco. Afterwards we were going to the wine country with another couple for a few days. My wife, who hasn't even had a cold in the last ten years, evidently contracted the flu during the convention and had to be taken to the emergency room. She

THE HORSEMAN'S GUIDE TO THE MEANING OF LIFE